TALK 2 MORE PEOPLE

Dear Vera,
Thankyou for the excellent work that you do in this world. I hope that you enjoy my book, and I look forward to seeing you again soon.

CHANGE YOUR LIFE BY MEETING PEOPLE

Yours in connection,

Tony Esteves

TONY ESTEVES

Talk2MorePeople Books
Calgary, Alberta, Canada
Talk2MorePeople.com

ISBN 978-1-7774362-0-9 (paperback)
ISBN 978-1-7774362-1-6 (ebook)
ISBN 978-1-7774362-2-3 (audiobook)

Editing by Erin Parker
Cover and interior design by Palmo Carpino
Ebook conversion by Bright Wing Media
Project management by Carra Simpson

Printed and bound in Canada

CONTENTS

"Reflecting deepens learning and reveals much beauty."

INTRODUCTION

THE IMPORTANCE OF IN-PERSON CONNECTIONS TODAY _____

"I feel the impulse but hesitate. And then the opportunity is gone. I wanted to say hello, to ask a question, to start a conversation, but I didn't. That's okay. They probably would have thought that I was a weirdo anyhow. What would I have said?"

Does this sound familiar? This is the same internal monologue I heard when I was afraid to meet people. I didn't know that they'd appreciate meeting me and that so many incredible new friendships, business relationships, and experiences were waiting to happen for me. If I'd understood what was possible when I was younger, I would have just taken the chance and spoken up. I would have started to talk to more people sooner.

Conversations between strangers create a ripple effect of positivity. This positivity starts when people connect for the first time and it expands within each individual. Then it ripples out to the people in their networks.

Sometimes the real beauty in these seemingly chance interactions with new people lies in who it affects beyond the initial interaction. What new, different path did you choose to walk down as a result of your conversation? Who did you bump into along the way? What insight came from that unexpected connection? Did you find that you slowed down and became present? How did the person you met implement what you shared with them? Who did they share that information with?

The effects of an encounter with somebody new often extend far beyond our expectations. This can lead to real-world positive change for people who were not even involved in the initial interaction. Amazingly, it all starts with a simple face-to-face conversation between two people.

My intention is to share with you how easy it can be to improve your circumstances when you share a goal, dream, or simple idea with the person next to you. It doesn't matter where this happens. Interactions like this occur at the grocery store, in cafés, on transit, and in countless other places where we are surrounded by real, live people. They also happen in unexpected settings that make you feel that life is chuckling or winking at you.

Wouldn't it be handy to have a process to bring a new person into your life whenever you want? Of course it would. How about a functional grab bag of simple concepts and phrases that can make this challenging task manageable and even enjoyable? That's what is in store for you here. As humans, we have a natural desire to connect with other people.[1] We are social animals. We need to communicate with other humans. You can learn how to meet people, and you can learn to do it well (even if you are shaking your head doubtfully as you read this now). I was extremely introverted until my late teens and somehow became comfortable meeting strangers. No matter what stage of your life you are in now, you can too.

WHY BOTHER?

There are several convincing reasons why you should learn how to meet people. It is good for your mental health, for the people you reach out to, and for overall wellness. Do it for yourself, for your community, or for both. Learning how to approach and engage with strangers is an often-overlooked form of self-improvement. Social psychologist Gillian Sandstrom has proven that meeting strangers is good for your mood. According to Sandstrom, "We put our best face forward when we're talking to someone we don't know; we're on our best behaviour."[2]

Research suggests that merely approaching someone you don't know will make you feel better.

How refreshing an idea is that? Research suggests that merely approaching someone you don't know will make you feel better, particularly if you were in a bad mood before. And it's likely that the person whom you approached will feel better too. What a way to cheer up. If you knew that speaking to a stranger would improve two people's day, would you make more attempts at it?

Can you imagine a world where everybody reaches out to connect with strangers? It could be a world where people continuously exchange ideas and resources with one another, just like friends, whether they know each other or not. It may sound overly optimistic, but pockets of social activity like this already exist.

Intentionally meeting new people is your opportunity to help co-create that world. Simple, brief exchanges with strangers have the potential to change the course of a person's life, or even save one. It also addresses the current epidemic of loneliness on our planet.

I encourage you to throw yourself into this learning experience. Expect to succeed, fall, flop, be pleasantly surprised, very occasionally feel rejected, and eventually, transform! If you take action with the materials presented in this book, you will be rewarded for your efforts beyond the limits of your imagination.

Well done for making this investment in yourself and exploring the idea that human connection is more important today than ever before (even while limited to online interaction). By doing so, you are giving yourself and the world the great gift of a beautiful, adventurous opportunity. You are helping increase the vitally important global human connection. In time you may even become an advocate for creating this ripple effect of positivity. Welcome to Talk2MorePeople.

WHAT STOPS US

Many factors keep people from reaching out to others to create a face-to-face connection. Here we will touch on three of the most common obstacles that I have observed and talked to people about: fear of rejection, being over-connected, and fear of change.

We Fear Rejection

Nobody wants to feel rejected. Many people exhibit a fear of rejection throughout their lives. Do you?[3]

It is entirely reasonable to fear rejection. It is often linked to our fear of experiencing pain, disappointment, and hurt. This fear can extend into many areas of our lives and is often the reason for not attempting to connect with new people at all.

When you're making an important decision, you may feel a little uneasy with an option that points you in a new direction or deposits you in unfamiliar territory. That option is often the path of growth. Choosing to put yourself in uncomfortable (but not dangerous) situations can accelerate your development in many areas of your life. Meeting new people is one way to practise overcoming discomfort and growing from it. Unfortunately, we have been conditioned to believe that it's not safe to meet new people, and therefore we avoid it.

The fear of rejection stops us from choosing the uncomfortable situation, so we miss opportunities that could help us grow. Regarding meeting people, it stops us from saying hello or asking a question when it comes to mind. Instead, we overthink the situation and decide that we would get rejected, so we don't bother trying. This is a costly mistake.

Suppose statistics proved that getting rejected when approaching a stranger is far less common than you think? Suppose research showed that almost every time you initiate a conversation with a stranger, they think more highly of you than you expect?

In their now-famous series of studies, "Mistakenly Seeking Solitude," researchers Nicholas Epley and Juliana Schroeder show how people on Chicago trains and buses who connected with a stranger on their commute felt better afterwards: "Commuters on a train into downtown Chicago reported a significantly more positive commute when they connected with a stranger than when they sat in solitude, and yet they predicted precisely the opposite pattern of experiences. This pattern of results demonstrates a severe misunderstanding of the psychological consequences of social engagement."[4] The researchers duplicated their studies in the UK with very similar findings.[5] When you engage with people on a commute, you are unlikely to get rejected, and you are very likely to enjoy the engagement more than you thought you would.

Unfortunately, most people don't know about these studies, and they continue to hold the false belief that we are happier to remain in solitude while commuting and in many other public situations. But we can get past this. It takes the willingness to intentionally meet new people and the effort to learn this skill.

I love people, and yet I too have a fear of rejection. It's just far weaker than it used to be. I have approached thousands of strangers, and less than 2 percent have entirely rejected me, looked at me like I had three eyes, or seemed inconvenienced. None of those rejections was hurtful. It is extremely rare to be denied when you approach strangers tactfully.

If you do get bounced out of a conversation or are unable to join one, don't take it personally. There are so many factors at play in any social situation that it's difficult to know for sure if the issue was your approach or something you said. So don't be too hard on yourself. That being said, be sure to visit the chapter "Uncomfortable? How to Exit a Conversation," which provides guidelines for you so you can be certain that you are not making someone else uncomfortable—which nobody wants.

By getting past the fear of rejection, we gain access to more opportunities to learn new things, connect with new people in meaningful ways, and expand our social networks. If you are up for it, you could take a swing at rejection therapy to beat this fear, or you could simply play with the tools and techniques you'll see in the pages coming up.[6] Expect to enjoy the developments that unfold in your life.

We Are Over-Connected

Face-to-face encounters with strangers are bursting with the potential to transform lives; however, much of this potential often gets overlooked. We are so busy responding to our digital devices that it can be easy to forget that people surround us much of the time—Ping! How many notifications did you get while reading these first few pages?—and are our most excellent resource.

If you feel that people are getting lost in technology today and you find it challenging to make new connections in person, you are not alone. Ask two random people if they think we are over-connected digitally and you will get at least one yes. Our society's zombification by devices is, by coincidence, a handy conversation starter. However, it's not enough to only acknowledge that there is a problem.

The solution is to learn how to meet people and how to better manage time with technology—important soft skills. Many people don't know that they have a choice to be less digitally connected, so they have never tried it. And research proves that receiving notifications reduces productivity, even if you don't look at them immediately.[7] Letting go of the tendency to be over-connected can be uncomfortable at first, especially since much of the world transitioned to doing just about everything online in 2020.

But it is still possible to digitally disconnect. On a day off, see if you can get through four or more hours without going online at all. If reading that sentence made you twitch uncomfortably, aim for just a couple hours off of the devices. To begin with, it may seem painful, or like a part of you is missing, but the more that you do it, the more opportunities you will have to build human connection. You may even feel it's liberating and eventually decide to have one offline day per week. Maybe you will experiment with a "no devices day" with your family. Of course, you might be thinking, *I need to be responsive. I can't go offline for that long because so much of my work is virtual.* Fair enough. In that case, consider when in the week you are not on the clock. Be curious and notice how being so wired affects your well-being and stress level. Then explore if you can create more time to be offline. Putting down the phone, tablet, or latest mind-reading wearable technology may not seem like a productive use of your time, but it can be far more beneficial long term than you might know. The results of catching up on a few emails or texts while standing in line are finite. However, the possible outcomes from meeting a new person are infinite. An interaction with just one new person has the potential to change the direction of your life!

"But I *am* talking to people, just online." Does that sound familiar? Of course you are. Everybody's on the internet now. In 2019 there were 4.388 billion internet users for a penetration of 57 percent of the global population. And of those billions of people, 45 percent of them were active social media users.[8] Now, that is a lot of people who are using the internet to "connect." But in doing so, many people compare themselves to other people online, and this causes negative self-esteem and a host of other problems.

An interaction with just one new person has the potential to change the direction of your life!

Unfortunately, studies have shown a correlation between social media use and loneliness. But this also provides an opportunity. People can benefit by limiting their social media activity. A 2018 study from the University of Pennsylvania found "experimentally limiting social media usage on a mobile phone to ten minutes per platform per day for a full three weeks had a significant impact on well-being. Both loneliness and depressive symptoms declined in the experimental group... The results from our experiment strongly suggest that limiting social media usage does have a direct and positive impact on subjective well-being over time, especially with respect to decreasing loneliness and depression."[9]

We can reduce loneliness and depression by limiting how much time we spend on social media. Even merely monitoring how much time we spend on social media helps people reduce their usage.

We can also monitor the statistics that our devices provide for us. When we become aware of how much time we spend online, we can begin to change that behaviour if necessary.

So if you know that you, too, are currently over-connected, don't worry. You are not alone in this modern world. And you will find resources in this book to help you digitally disconnect. Here is an old-fashioned idea that works. Add in more face-to-face conversations to your life and regain control of your time.

We Fear Change

Does change excite you or make you uncomfortable? Change can be scary. If you are comfortable with your routine, and sometimes even if you don't like it, the idea of inviting a new item into your itinerary may be unwelcome or rejected.

So you walk away from opportunities to meet new people because you don't "do change." It's never been your thing. Perhaps you identify strongly with the discipline around your routine. It's part of who you are. It's part of why you are so productive.

No problem. I understand. There can be a strong sense of security when you know what to expect on any given day. But this is a gentle reminder that change can be just what you need.

In the *Psychology Today* article "How to Overcome the Fear of Change," Gustavo Razzetti, author of *Stretch for Change,* writes, "On one hand, we are hardwired to resist uncertainty—our brain prefers a predictable, negative outcome over an uncertain one. On the other hand, our mind is flexible and adaptive—it can be trained to thrive in change."[10] But many people are unaware that they can learn to thrive in change.

What if the reason you "don't do change" is because you never considered that your situation could be much better? What if by adding change into your routine, you could incrementally—and still with a sense of control—bring more activities, experiences, and people into your life? Would you consider it then?

There is no need to fear change because it is something that all people must deal with throughout life. It can be severe and dramatic, or it can be subtle. It can be heart-wrenching or lead to states of pure bliss.

So as you navigate this Talk2MorePeople journey, please keep in mind that the discomfort you may feel about changing your behaviour will likely be very good for your personal and professional development. And for now, you don't need to change a thing. You just need to remain open.

MY STORY

Before we explore some of the tools that make talking to strangers easier, I want to share some of the things that used to stop me from having conversations and the benefits I've enjoyed since getting past these obstacles. This is how I grew from a shy kid to the author of a book about talking to more people.

Dear Old Dad

A Portuguese immigrant to Canada in 1958, my late father, Antonio (Tony) Joaquim Esteves, was as European as could be in spirit and character. On the job site, Tony could be surly and rough to work with, but he had a heart of gold. He knew everybody in the neighbourhood and was always working on projects in the garage. He was a general contractor by trade and could take apart and fix just about anything mechanical. He would tinker on objects as small as a watch to as large as a diesel engine in his spare time.

Ours was one of those garages where much living happened. However, it wasn't just for working on cars, loading the truck with tools, or building. It was also for making wine, eating food, being creative, and constructing toys. Traditional Portuguese music or Johnny Cash often blared on an old radio. The garage was messy, oily, and littered with hazards that no child should have ever been around. I loved it. It was the kind of industrial zoo where only he knew where everything was, much to my frustration as his helper. It had the smell of a machine shop, and I now feel nostalgic when visiting a mechanic's garage. As the only boy in the family, this was my playground. It was a place where I could get my hands dirty building and using power tools that were not mother-approved. He had the mindset "If you burn yourself or get a shock, you won't do it again." And he was right. Sudden jolts of unexpected pain were a great teacher, as they are in life.

The garage was also for speaking with all kinds of people as well as sharing life-learning experiences. If you grew up in North America with parents from abroad, this might sound familiar. Many of us knew of or visited such industrial social hubs. For some unknown reason, it can be comforting to share stories and personal growth around machinery and unfinished industrial crafts. At least that's how it was for my father and me. He didn't talk about feelings, but our garage was always open to the community for the business of getting to know people.

Many diverse people walked through that garage door. They would stop by to visit, borrow tools, or work on a project. Cousins, neighbours of all ethnicities, and even strangers would stop in to get their lawn mowers or kids' bicycles fixed, for example. He knew so many people. He helped so many people. We could have hung a sign over the garage that said, "Everyone welcome. Come on in! Let's talk."

When someone had a problem or needed something fixed, he would stop what he was working on and state confidently, "No problem!" Then he would turn his attention to helping in any way that he could. In the neighbourhood, he wouldn't always get people's names right. If he didn't know yours, he'd just give you a random name, and use that. He would speak at length with anyone who would listen. Doing so was part of his friendly and curious nature.

Observing this growing up as a quiet child had an impact on me because I saw the benefits of talking to people before my own eyes. New friendships began, people helped each other out, and a sense of community was always there. It was good for me as a kid to be around this. My parents were quite social, and it just seemed normal that people would talk to one another so much, and so often.

How many people or adventures did I miss because I spent several hours a day looking at the screen?

Despite this, I lived a very introverted life until my late teens. Talking to all kinds of people was something that I thought only adults did. I was a shy child and kept to myself. Between the ages of thirteen and twenty-three, I played hundreds of hours of video games—not online but using cartridges or CDs. Remember those? I never thought of myself as addicted to gaming, though I guess for a while I was. Online games today are far more sophisticated and social than video games were in the '80s, but I still believe that there is no substitute for an in-person exchange between two people. In person, you get to learn important life skills like "how to not feel super-awkward." How many people or adventures did I miss because I spent several hours a day looking at the screen?

In my late teens, I began to develop the social skills that I had seen my father exhibit. For starters, I became more talkative and outspoken. I was also inspired in high school by my three sisters to use my voice and I looked up to each of them. (I still do.) Gradually, I began to speak my mind out loud and got involved with student leadership. This helped me get out of my shell and into university. Three years later, with a communications degree but no job and plenty of debt, I followed a friend out to Canada's west coast, British Columbia.

That first flight of my life marked the beginning of several years of international travel that had a profound impact on my life. The impact was so deep for me and so connected to meeting people that I'll share more details of this international journey in "The Traveller" chapter of the Mindset section.

While on the move, I followed work and adventure while meeting beautiful people everywhere I looked. Random conversations literally took me places. This travel was my informal education. Yet, as stimulating and eye-opening as travelling is, after eight years of moving around, this began to nag at me: I couldn't figure out what to do with my life more than a few months in advance. It's a bit of a traveller's paradox: the experiences look and are, in fact, excellent, but the life clock still ticks on.

Have you felt the negativity of stress, frustration, anger, or financial insecurity while observers express, "Oh, your life is such a dream"? Have you felt guilty for still trying to figure out what to do with your life late into your twenties, thirties, or beyond? If so, you are not alone. Each of these negative emotions have had starring roles in my story. In 2010, it became clear that no amount of travel or exciting experiences could break my negative cycles of behaviour. My inner spark had gone out.

I had been dealing with several mental health challenges for many years by then. My depression, angry outbursts, and occasional self-harming incidents—that I kept a secret from everyone—were becoming more frequent. Thankfully my partner at the time, Heather, and my twin sister Andrea advised me to get into therapy.

I had the stubborn attitude "I don't need to see a therapist!" Avoiding help allowed me to dodge the deep fear that something was wrong with me. Although it was unhealthy, I revelled in the comforting familiarity of suffering. Sometimes when we're hurting, we're not in the right heart- or headspace to get out of that darkness and look towards the positive, never mind trying something new. But something new could be precisely what we need. Life can be gentle, bursting with beauty, generosity, abundance, and even a wonderful adventure, when we are ready to receive it.

All therapists are not compatible with all people, but the second psychotherapist I met with was a good fit for me. I began to understand why I thought the way I did and was attracting specific experiences in my life. I started living healthier and stopped beating myself up. Therapy also taught me how to be a better listener and support for others.

I gained control of my thoughts and emotions and became more functional at work. It dramatically reduced but didn't completely get rid of the angry outbursts. One such incident in 2015 almost cost me my life. This scare led me to try antidepressants, which I'd previously avoided like cats do swimming pools. But they helped me, and the angry outbursts stopped; I was numb to extreme lows and highs.

A year passed on antidepressants. I needed something to help me get out of bed in the morning. Having not travelled for ages, I wanted something to be passionate and excited about once again.

The Talk2MorePeople Project

Intuitively knowing that meeting strangers has significant benefits, I decided to start a social experiment I called The Talk2MorePeople Project. It was a challenge to meet at least one stranger every single day for thirty days—no matter how I was feeling—to see what would happen.

I set out to meet at least one new stranger a day for a full year.

Many things happened! With very little clue of what I was doing or how daunting it might be, I went for it and was bountifully supported. The kind, creative, passionate, and generous people whom I met in that month showed me the beauty of humanity. There were brief chats, in-depth conversations, and dreamy escapades.

With the advice of my business coach, I extended the thirty-day challenge to 365 days. She said, "Tony, if you want to make an impact with this, don't do it for a month. Do it for a year." Thanks, Karin, for that timely and outrageous suggestion. Sometimes we need a friend who believes in us to boldly present a ridiculous challenge that takes our minds off our troubles.

So with that, I set out to meet at least one new stranger a day for a full year.

I wanted to become a physically and mentally healthier person and genuinely wished to Talk2MorePeople out of curiosity and playfulness. I intended to prove that there are great benefits from taking a break from technology and engaging in face-to-face conversations with strangers.

The project goals evolved as the project went on:

- Have fun meeting new people
- Learn new things
- Be heard and seen
- Improve my life situation
- Have new, random experiences
- Encourage others to look up from their phones and meet people
- Get more work
- See what would happen

It began in London, England, in April 2016.[11] Almost immediately, I began to feel my vitality and zest for life re-emerge. The new, positive energy and a little fate led me into an adventure with Sylvie, whom I met on Day 10 while in Italy. She and I travelled together for five days in France, which was a beautiful, spontaneous surprise that I will forever be grateful for. I visited friends in Spain and family in Canada, and the project wrapped up in Calgary, Alberta, one year later.

The Talk2MorePeople Project became my reason to get out of bed in the morning. It was my opportunity to explore first-hand the benefits of talking to and helping strangers that I had witnessed so often growing up as that shy boy. The project allowed me to create a community like I had seen in that garage decades earlier.

Reacquainted with my authentic, playful self, I got my spark back. It was like a switch had been turned back on within me. But this time, it wasn't about the instant stimulation and gratification that travelling can provide. More in-depth than that, it was about relationships and human connection.

I was able to showcase the benefits of meeting people face to face by documenting my experiences through writing, short videos, and photos on the Talk2MorePeople Facebook page. The social media portion of the project was conflicting. I got the desired sense of accomplishment from posting daily updates and reading comments but also felt I was being held hostage by how much time it took to keep up. Just like raising cute little pigs, social media is a beast that has an insatiable appetite. You can keep feeding it, but it never seems to get full. And at times it's worth asking, "Do I really need to feed this beast now?"

My life expanded with new social engagements, invitations, and activities. I learned about new communities of people that, before the project, I didn't know existed. Within these communities, I attended house concerts, acrobatic yoga classes, parties, and music festivals. I encountered fascinating people and new ideas. Have you ever really thought about what positive activities your city or town has to offer? Curiosity and exploration can change your life.

A meeting with a stranger even led me to join the circus!

As you can imagine, Talk2MorePeople encounters happened at business events, in cafés, and while on public transportation. But they also occurred in unexpected places. I met Bill and Terri while in the hospital on Day 309; Amy at a red light in the cycling lane on Day 142; and Mike the internet service provider in my living room on Day 365.

The opportunities that I gained access to gave me the confidence to scale back and ultimately get off medication. I met mentors, community leaders, and new colleagues to collaborate with. I landed more work for my business, which put bread on the table. I met individuals who increased my awareness of the challenges for Indigenous people in Canada today. I learned from academics and played with professional athletes and extraordinary musicians. I got out of a rut and started dating. I hiked with hikers and drank with drinkers. I met lads who would become roommates. A meeting with a stranger even led me to join the circus!

It was so much fun. I'll share more of these stories over the course of the book, but for now it's enough to say that intentionally meeting more than 550 new people in one year was the most significant and rewarding challenge I had ever undertaken. I continue to celebrate the benefits of those new connections, both personally and professionally. And beyond the relationships, the memories that have been co-created through shared experience have enriched my life beyond measure.

Meeting people helped me regain control of my life; I believe it will do the same for you.

The inspiration for starting this project—that eventually led me to better mental health, social connectedness, and happiness—goes back to my talkative, helpful Portuguese father in my childhood garage. I observed the basics while young, though it took me years to use what I had learned. But you don't need years to learn this stuff.

Now, how can my experience help you?

HOW THIS BOOK WILL HELP YOU

The stories and process in this book will take you on a journey. If you have been reading with curiosity, you will have guessed by now that it's a journey of in-person human connection. Meaningful new connections can also begin online in today's virtual world, however that is not the focus here. Drawing upon research and real-life experiences from multiple sources, this book will help you by illustrating that talking to strangers is a worthwhile skill to learn. And it will also teach you how to meet people. If all goes as planned, you'll relate to it in a way that inspires, pesters, prompts, and prepares you to go meet new people and get a taste or, if you prefer, a buffet of the sweetness that this life has to offer. *Bon appétit* and *bon voyage.*

As in most books, the content has been laid out to be read from start to finish. But as I'm speaking to you now from the page, screen, speaker, or headset, you already know my brain far better than I know yours. So you'll know best in what order you would most like to consume Talk2MorePeople. If there's a section that grabs your attention, go there now. Part 2, "The LOOKUP Process for Meeting People" will be most digestible if you read it in order. But otherwise, follow the shiny object.

If you see a section or a tip or tool that speaks to you, use it the same day. Don't wait to complete the book before attempting to use a technique. Get out there and practise while the information is fresh in your mind. That's one way to reinforce learning.

In Part 1, you will find four mindsets to prepare you for the journey:

The Child: *Be Curious and Spontaneous*

The Meditator: *Be Present*

The Traveller: *Be Adventurous*

The Juggler: *Be Adaptable*

You may be able to relate to one or more of these mindsets already. Consciously bringing them into your life at a time when you want to meet people will guarantee that more connections come your way. In each of the mindset chapters, I'll provide an explanation of the mindset, the challenges and benefits possible from applying it, and finally tips on how to embrace it. Each of the mindsets will be referred to throughout the book, so get ready, set, mindset!

In Part 2, we'll work through the "LOOKUP Process for Meeting People." The acronym LOOKUP makes each step easy to remember:

L: Listen
O: Overcome Internal Obstacles
O: Open a Dialogue—Six Strategies
K: Keep (the Conversation) Going
U: Uncomfortable? How to Exit a Conversation
P: Play and Improvise

The acronym LOOKUP is also used as a helpful reminder that much of the disconnect in society today could be solved if people literally *looked up* from their devices more often to see and interact with the real world. At the time of writing, people spend, on average, over four hours per day looking at phones.[12] The world of information is now at our fingertips, and a striking amount of business takes place on these devices. But what is the cost of giving screens more attention than the people whom we are surrounded by—both at home and in public? The cost is enormous and creating systemic problems in how we communicate as adults today, how our children's brains develop, and how we become socialized.[13] To stop doing more damage, we need to talk more and put the devices down. We need to have more conversations. And we don't have to depend only on philosophical, profound discussions. Simple, seemingly mundane interactions between strangers also have the power to create a significant, positive impact.

Life is packed with adventure, but only when you are open to it.

You can use this six-step process to make these conversations happen, whether you meet people as often as you eat or as infrequently as you celebrate birthdays.

In Part 3, "Success Stories," you will hear from a number of fine people who I've met through random conversations. Each shares a meaningful story of how meeting a stranger had a positive impact on them.

At the end of the book, you will find other resources that have made an impact on me that you may choose to explore if your curiosity level has gone up. They'll allow you to dig deeper into the art of meeting new people. While you will pick up the basics of mindfulness from "The Meditator" mindset chapter, I've asked an expert—my friend and colleague Tracey Delfs—to provide a more in-depth mindfulness menu for you to enjoy in the Appendix.

So, why Talk2MorePeople? By navigating this process, you will have new, positive encounters that will surprise and enlighten you. These experiences will be random and unpredictable, reconnecting you with the true essence of play and the beauty of living a full life. Such experiences can lead to growth unlike anything your life has presented to you before. Talk2MorePeople is a proven new method to once again connect to your true inner self and other people. Life is packed with adventure, but only when you are open to it.

What is your inspiration to connect? Is it an inspiring friend or family member, the urge to find work or more human connection, or the desire to experience more adventure? Can you imagine what opportunities and gifts might be just on the horizon for you?

Take this model and make it your own. Any suit or costume you try on will be most comfortable when small alterations have been made to custom-fit your body. The same applies to many ideas. Keep in mind that through this process it's okay to drop the ball. Learning any new skill will involve messing up along the way. To begin with, it may be challenging. But you will soon discover that intentionally meeting new people is empowering and even great fun.

To expand your social world, and to bring more opportunities, experiences, and people into your life, all you need to do is look up and talk to more people.

KEY TERMS AND CONCEPTS

There are a few unique terms that will appear throughout the book, so here's an introduction.

What Is a Talk2MorePeople Encounter?

A Talk2MorePeople Encounter happens when you learn something from a stranger or they learn something from you. It's that simple.

Have you ever asked for directions in public? Have you ever helped someone or answered a person's question in public?

Has someone random ever recommended a movie that you eventually watched? If so, you have experienced Talk2MorePeople encounters already. In fact, unless you have been fully isolated your entire life, you have had many. Asking for or sharing news or resources during casual conversation is a part of how we regularly communicate in our day-to-day lives. It is part of how we navigate this world, so it can come naturally to anyone. And the initial social encounter could last for just a few moments or for several hours. Sometimes you won't even exchange names. Regardless of length, it can lead to a lifetime friendship or partnership. Believe it or not, Talk2MorePeople encounters happen all the time.

The Information Gift Exchange

At the end of an interaction between two strangers, at least one person has something in their brain that was not there before. This could be a simple concept or something elaborate and mind-bending. This is an Information Gift Exchange.

Conversing with another person and sharing that time together face to face in itself is a gift because it is an opportunity to grow human connection. The ideas and information exchanged lead to real-world change once people take action on what they learn. Be open to offering your gifts through conversation and be open to receiving them as well.

Of course, you won't always be interested in attending the event, climbing the mountain, or travelling to the obscure place mentioned in conversation. You may not want to buy the book, take the course, sponsor the cause, or do whatever the information gift exchange entails. And that's totally fine. Just because somebody gives you a gift, it doesn't mean that you have to open it.

Even if you don't make use of the information you've exchanged, you can still brighten the person's day by simply acknowledging them and communicating with them, and this is also a gift. Doing so can lead to greater happiness and to making more positive decisions that will, in turn, have a better effect on the people with whom they interact on any given day. Ultimately, that is the greatest information gift exchange of all: the unknown ripple effects of positivity to other people that result from the time you spend interacting with a stranger.

Below are three examples of an information gift exchange.

Example One: Share a Website Resource

Let's say that a person tells you about an interesting website in conversation. At that moment, you could choose to take five seconds to look up the address or save a note about it, rather than brush it off. Who knows where it might lead you? Websites can be portals to other worlds.

Have you ever discovered a website that fits your interests perfectly and thought, *Yes! Finally, this is for me*? Exploring a body of knowledge that you didn't know existed can be life-changing. Good websites can be magical places where mountains of information live, ready to be interacted with and consumed. Sharing a website is one way that the information gift exchange happens all the time. It's non-threatening and has practical utility.

There are many resources mentioned throughout the book and conveniently gathered in the Other Resources section. Please check them out and share them with others once you find something useful.

> You don't need a script to connect with people; you only need to be willing to share the value that is already within you.

Example Two: Share a Book Title

Books are amazing. The good ones are insightful and occasionally entertaining or inspirational collections of words ordered usefully. Sharing the title of a book that had an impact on you with someone you meet at an event, while in line, at work, or in transit is an information gift exchange. The other person might take note of this and download or purchase that book as a result of your recommendation. When a reader is connected with an appropriate book that is relevant to them, transformation can occur.

Can you think of a book that has changed your life? Why not share the knowledge that you have with the people you meet? It won't cost you a thing and has the potential create so much positivity. You don't need a script to connect with people; you only need to be willing to share the value that is already within you.

Example Three: Share Details About an Event
Two people meet in line at the grocery store. The first person comments to the other, "Hey, that's a lot of hot dog buns that you have there." The second person responds, "They're for a festival that I am heading to this weekend. Do you want to hear about it?"

In this brief exchange, the first person learns about a local festival that he had never heard of before. He then chooses to attend the festival and by doing so meets an entirely new community of like-minded people who become his friends and peer support group. His efforts to connect with a stranger changes his life. Such rewards are within reach for us every day.

These are examples of how even a little bit of effort and a seemingly small piece of information can lead to significant, real-world change. It is not only about sharing information about a book, website, or event, but also ideas. By sharing an idea with another person—you create the possibility for positive change both within yourself and the other individual. The act of speaking about your idea to another person adds energy to that idea and can help bring it to fruition. It is as if you are fertilizing intellectual seeds by interacting with people out there in the real world.

There are so many gifts to be explored through information exchange. But where to begin? Begin by being open to *this* idea. Begin by looking up and reaching out. More details on the specifics of such interactions are ahead.

Juggle the Conversation

I am a professional performer and have been juggling since last century. Juggling is near and dear to me as it has helped me meet dozens of people over the years. The idea of "Juggling the Conversation" can help you too.

While learning the steps of how to juggle three balls, people often think that it's impossible. But with clear instructions, and by breaking it into manageable steps, they soon realize that they can do it. Later in the process, there is an interesting phenomenon. The student can accelerate their learning by jumping to three balls before they've mastered catching two. It often works because the more difficult task makes the earlier step unconsciously happen. There is stretching, sometimes frustration, and always growth. The seemingly impossible task becomes possible before their own eyes.

The same is true when learning how to meet people. There are many different factors to consider at the same time and it can seem overwhelming. Following clear instructions and tackling the process in manageable steps (also on the way), you too will realize that it is possible. Even if you don't feel ready and even if, at first, it doesn't work, pushing yourself to strike up a conversation is an admirable task. And it can accelerate your growth because you skip past some of your old inhibitions by making the attempt.

When you contribute to a discussion, you will be juggling the conversation, with all of its beautiful and challenging unpredictability. Use the resources that you have within and around you to help make a conversation last longer and go deeper.

Both juggling and a conversation with a stranger have these things in common: They are challenging skills that you can learn; they can be simple or complex; failures lead to successes; while juggling or talking, you can lose track of time; they require patience and repetition in order for you to become competent; and they are extremely fun and rewarding.

For an insightful book on how to juggle as well as learn how to learn, read *Lessons from the Art of Juggling* by Michael Gelb and Tony Buzan. They write at length about the "art of relaxed concentration," an excellent state to be in while meeting new people. It is all about development when learning to juggle balls or a conversation; the more that you do it, the easier it will become.

T2MP Day What?

There are a number of references to "T2MP Day (number)" throughout the book. This is a short form to represent the numbered days of the 365-day Talk2MorePeople Project. Plug #T2MP into the internet to see or share fun research and stories on human connection.

 MINDSETS

These four mindsets have played a role in the thousands of interactions I've had with strangers, so I thought it would be useful to include them here. By embracing these mindsets, you may begin to notice benefits beyond success in meeting new people, such as increased happiness, more joy and play, more adventure, and overall wellness. Take a dive in here, see what you can relate to, and keep these mindsets in mind as they pop up from time to time on the page and in your life.

THE CHILD: BE CURIOUS AND SPONTANEOUS _____

To be more childlike, you don't have to give up being an adult. The fully integrated person is capable of being both an adult and a child simultaneously. Recapture the childlike feelings of wide-eyed excitement, spontaneous appreciation, cutting loose, and being full of awe and wonder at this magnificent universe.
—Wayne Dyer

One summer day, my partner and I were enjoying outrageously large homemade salads on a bench in a park in Kelowna, British Columbia. It was quiet and empty. Suddenly about fifteen children were unleashed on the playground from a bus and it was pandemonium. They looked like a class of seven-year-olds who had just had lots of ice cream. The energy was sky-high. It was a delight to see. What was so enjoyable to witness was how easily and spontaneously the kids created stories and games wherever they interacted. They were clearly curious about their surroundings and each other while playing. Some were spinning in the swings like helicopters, for example. While climbing on a giant, metal, ant-like structure, two other kids were talking to it like they were friends, being creative and using their imaginations. It was beautiful.

We can learn a great deal from these curious, spontaneous, little monsters. That sense of curiosity, spontaneity, and play is not only great for developing fundamental social skills as a child but also for connecting with people as adults.[14]

Why Be Curious?

Are you curious about people? Or are you not so bothered? When you take a moment and observe someone who you know can't see you, do you ever wonder what they are thinking? Do you ever dare to ask?

Curiosity is great for your mind and the development of your brain.[15] The benefits can extend into your career as well. Even if you are not so curious about approaching a stranger and would rather drink a glass of sand, sit tight. You might soon give yourself a chance to grow your curiosity. Being curious is a child-like quality that is in each of us, but we may not explore it as adults. Part of the Child's Mindset is that it is a critical aspect of meeting new people. As Jane Fonda says, "Stay curious. It's much more important to stay interested than to be interesting."[16] You don't need to try to flaunt your skills. The best thing you can do is genuinely show an interest in what the other person or people are sharing with you.

Living without curiosity is like having tunnel vision while squinting your eyes. It prohibits you from seeing opportunities just on the periphery of your life experience. You don't have to be a wildly curious person to meet strangers, but a little curiosity is required. Stacks of curiosity are quite advantageous.

If you can practise being more curious about the world around you, you can learn how to meet people. A healthy measure of curiosity (more like a child's and less like an adult's level) provides useful insights on how to create conversations that will connect you to people. The more curious you can become, the easier it will be.

Why Do Adults Lose Their Sense of Curiosity?

Life gets hectic! Adults collect more and more responsibilities as time goes on while children are free to play. Curiosity can get stifled with the clutter of day-to-day tasks, and we believe there is no time to explore our creative interests. In our busy lives, we can dismiss curiosity as unimportant, or it may not seem to fit in with whatever industry we work in. As Francesca Gino says in "The Business Case for Curiosity," "Despite the well-established benefits of curiosity, organizations often discourage it."[17] And sometimes, we simply don't even think about it.

Routine can be helpful and healthy; however, too much of it can be problematic. You may not even be aware that you have a choice to explore your surroundings, environments, and people in your day-to-day life. What a shame. Even if there was no imminent danger, would you tell a child not to explore their surroundings? Over time, how might that limit their curiosity?

Benefits of Being Curious

Children are natural champions of curiosity. When you become curious, you open yourself up to countless possibilities. Here are just a few of the many benefits of being curious that relate to connecting with new people:[18]

- Curious people are happier.
- Curiosity can expand our empathy.
- Curiosity helps strengthen relationships.
- Curiosity allows you to follow your intuition more.
- Curiosity is mentally stimulating and rewarding.
- Curiosity makes you look up and around at your surroundings.
- Curiosity allows you to see detail, beauty and meaning in places that you've been before but not truly seen.
- Being curious is fun.

How Do We Get Our Curiosity Back?

Meeting more people will help you become more curious, and becoming more curious will help you meet more people. Shall we begin with the chicken or the egg? Jump into this virtuous cycle wherever you like to enjoy more of the benefits listed above.

Tips for Being More Curious

You can take small steps to increase the level of curiosity you experience or make it a lifelong pursuit. Below are a few tips to get you started:

- Take a new road, path, or method of transportation to work or school or wherever you go most often.

- Break your daily routine, even if it takes a little longer to complete tasks.

- Spend time in a new place.

- Read something different.

- Study a new language, and with that learn about a new culture.

- Call (don't text or email) someone you haven't spoken with for months or years.

- Observe children playing.

- Try an activity that you have never done before.

- Think about times in your life when you have already experienced being curious.

In conversations with new people, let your curiosity about what you see, feel, sense, and experience guide you. If you have the normal tendency to overthink while nervous, that is okay. Curiosity—like a helpful, invisible friend whispering hints in your ear—will tell you what to say when you're drawing a blank. But only if you are open to hearing it. Listen to the wisdom that your curiosity can provide.

Being genuinely curious will lead you to ask questions rather than to talk on and on about yourself. It will allow you to learn more from others and to more quickly find out how you could be of service to them even during a brief encounter.

Be Spontaneous

As we saw from the playground example above, children are naturally curious and spontaneous. These are both key elements to playing. As one child raced towards the swings, I saw him get easily sidetracked as some other game suddenly began elsewhere. He then spontaneously changed course and joined the other action. Isn't that what we all want as adults— permission to spontaneously follow the fun? This type of spontaneity invites opportunities to connect because it illustrates freedom within ourselves and to others. Emulating the child in this sense will guide you into the playful unknown.

So what does it mean to be spontaneous in the context of meeting more people?

Quite often, meeting new people happens without advance notice. By acting quickly and without overthinking the situation, you won't let these opportunities pass you by. Spontaneous people are able to go with the flow and react to the unexpected. Add a sprinkle of spontaneity to just about every technique offered in this book, and it will only improve your chances of connecting with people.

Spontaneity and adaptability are like friendly cousins—they are related. In "The Wisdom of Spontaneity (Part 2)," Leon Seltzer writes, "In essence, spontaneity is about adaptability and openness to change. It's about being willing to undertake new (or novel) behaviours when the 'tried and true' is ineffective or, frankly, has become boring."[19] This creates abundant opportunities for growth. Dare to act on impulse, and adventures await.

Obstacles to Being Spontaneous

When I ask, "Are you a spontaneous person?" you likely hear yourself answer a clear yes or no. No matter what you consider yourself to be now, what is it that stops so many of us from being spontaneous? See if any of these common obstacles apply in your case:

- Fear of embarrassment or failure
- Fear of offending someone
- Low self-esteem
- Uncertainty about how to use your own voice
- Miserably or happily stuck in routine
- Fear of the unknown
- Attachment to predictable outcomes
- Unawareness of the benefits of spontaneity

What if you found out that spontaneity was good for you? Would you suddenly feel empowered to be as spontaneous as you wanted? You would be able to live more of your life on your own terms. Maybe you would get closer to living the dream that other people talk about because you would have the courage to take risks and go for it. That would be nice, right? "So how do I become more spontaneous?" you ask? Let's have a look.

Tips to Be More Spontaneous

1. Say the First Thing That Comes to Mind

Listen to what your inner voice tells you, and without hesitation, say that! If it feels unnatural to say something that suddenly pops into your mind, this may be extremely uncomfortable. But isn't that a fantastic opportunity for growth? Getting the words out of your mouth and into the world is more possible when you don't think/worry about it so much.

People intuitively recognize authenticity and are attracted to it.

---

2. Believe Spontaneous Rewards Outweigh the Costs

What if someone doesn't like what you have to say? Well, that is a risk, yes. But if you keep your language clean and respectful, positive opportunities will arise. And at least you will develop a reputation for authenticity. See if you can channel that outspoken family member or awkward friend for a moment. Certainly they've offended people, but everyone who knows this person will agree that "they tell it like it is," and that's a good thing. It is honesty impulsively expressed out loud, and completely genuine. There is such a short time between when they make an observation, have the thought, and express it into words. My dear old dad was a pro at speaking his mind. Not everybody liked it, but everybody could agree that he was authentic because he spoke up spontaneously. Authenticity is connected to spontaneity. People intuitively recognize authenticity and are attracted to it.

3. Clear Your Schedule to Be More Spontaneous

Having a jam-packed schedule limits spontaneity.[20] I'll be the first to admit that I've overscheduled both my personal and professional life in the past. The results of doing so were high stress, a sense that I could never accomplish enough in a day, and very little room for spontaneity. Don't make the same mistake I made for many years. Leave room in your life for unexpected connections to unfold before you. You will be more relaxed and more present, and unplanned positive experiences will become a more regular part of your life.

Could you challenge yourself to be a little more spontaneous in the future to see what is possible? Here is an example of when I took the risk to spontaneously follow the fun as an adult.

In 2008, I joined a stranger for a bike ride. His name was Julian and he came from Germany. He'd found me through CouchSurfing—an online travellers' network—and was staying at my place. We cycled from Toronto to Vancouver together in forty-one days. Okay, it was a really long bike ride. It was both a spontaneous experience and a massive challenge. Returning from this trip, I was in great physical shape and ready to embark upon a much-needed career change. Sometimes a spontaneous adventure can be just what we need in life when the regular routine is no longer making us happy. It takes effort to overcome the obstacles, but the rewards can ultimately be *revolutionary* (obligatory cycling pun).

You don't need to be this extreme to be spontaneous when meeting new people. The most important thing is to simply be authentic. If you can allow yourself to say what you are thinking out loud more often—as I learned to do as a teenager—you will become more spontaneous. Knowing that great benefits await and allowing time in your schedule for the unknown will help you achieve this.

This doesn't mean that your life will suddenly become a wild adventure, but more adventures will find you. As a bonus, your self-esteem might get a boost as well.

An additional benefit to being both more curious and spontaneous is that you will also become more playful. That is another child-like quality that we will explore in the chapter "Play and Improvise."

THE MEDITATOR: BE PRESENT

If you are depressed, you are living in the past.
If you are anxious, you are living in the future.
If you are at peace, you are living in the present.
—*Lao Tzu*

Take a breath. When you reach out and invite another person into a conversation, you must be present to engage with what they have to say. Identifying and then practising your methods of becoming a more present person can make meeting people trouble-free.

Disclaimer: I am not an expert on being present, and I used to be the most scatter-brained busy-body I knew. I have, however, been fortunate to learn from wonderful people along the way and have apparently gotten pretty good at living in the moment. So I will share a sliver of a thought-pie on this topic here. Don't worry, the full pie will be on the table later.

What Does It Mean to Be Present?

Being present means not allowing your mind to tie your thoughts up in the past or the future. It means that you are not overly distracted or wishing that you were somewhere else. Even if you have thoughts racing around in your mind, when you are present, you are able to quiet those thoughts so that you can fully pay attention to whatever is going on around you. Being present can be managed with the breath.[21] Breath is a primary element for almost every meditation or yoga practice. When present, you have full access to your senses and body. You tap into your intuition and utilize all of your abilities to perform at a high level.

Learning to bring that same focus and attention to meeting new people will support you in this challenging but oh-so-rewarding endeavour.

Why Can't I Be Present?

Being present can be challenging, particularly if mindfulness is new to you. In our fast-paced, hyper-connected world, it can seem impossible to slow down and truly feel the present moment.

"I feel as though I'm always everywhere, except here." Does this sound familiar?

Have you ever felt guilty for not having a mindfulness practice? In my twenties and thirties, I experienced the benefits of meditation but still didn't do it regularly. I used to think that the only way to be mindful was through formal meditation. But during those years of travel—although I didn't know it—I was developing my informal mindfulness practice. Informal mindfulness practice is when you integrate mindfulness into daily activities. So, in fact, it can be for anyone. I didn't need to feel guilty for not meditating, and neither should you. You may have a strong informal mindfulness practice already.[22]

Hiking, juggling, cycling, performing, and reading are a few of my informal mindfulness practices. What are yours?

Benefits to Being Present

Practising being present is a worthwhile exercise on its own and it can also enable you to take on almost any challenge much more effectively. Some people claim that living in the present moment allows them to accomplish more in a day. By taking the time to practise mindfulness, the mind is clearer and, therefore, more gets done. It sounds counterintuitive, but it's true.[23]

If you ask any professional athlete or performer how they execute at such a high level, they will probably mention a ritual or mindfulness practice, or both. They may share how they have trained themselves to focus on the one specific moment they need to perform. Part of my ritual before a circus performance involves joking around with the costume and makeup crew before getting on stage. It primes me for action. I get ready to perform by using mindfulness.

Finally, being present connects you to gratitude. It allows you to more easily feel grateful for that which you already have but might not have acknowledged in the past. To truly appreciate the gift of life, slow down and express gratitude every day. You can feel grateful for anything from having eyes to read with to having access to food. Truthfully, gratitude can be felt for just about anything (even negative experience that fosters growth).

To truly appreciate the gift of life, slow down and express gratitude every day.

Below are a few tips to get you started.

Tips to Be More Present

Turn Off or Silence Your Technology, and Get It Out of Sight

Research has shown that the mere presence of a smartphone within sight negatively affects our ability to concentrate.[24] Experiment with physically distancing yourself from your device from time to time.

Breathe

Since you are doing it anyhow, why not just take deep breaths more consciously and more often? Many of us don't fully use our lungs and rely only on shallow breathing most of the day. You can take a few slow, deep breaths anywhere and anytime you need to shift your energy. Try it now and see how you feel.

Take the "One-Second Break"

This is a breathing technique that I offer in my workshops and can be used anytime. By stopping the action and taking one deep breath, participants can quickly return to the present moment.

Do the 5, 4, 3, 2, 1 Grounding Technique

Place a hand on your heart and use each of your senses to fully bring you into the present moment. This on its own can instantly reduce stress levels. This exercise creates a physiological response of calmness for most people because, as Linda Graham says in "Mitigate the Stress Response with a Hand on Your Heart," "The warm, safe touch of our hand on our heart centre begins to activate the release of oxytocin, the brain's hormone of safety and trust, bonding and belonging, calm and connect."[25] Why not allow the oxytocin to flow? Then take a deep breath and describe the following out loud:

- Look: Five objects that you can see
- Feel: Four sensations that you are experiencing in your body
- Listen: Three things that you can hear
- Smell: Two things that you can smell
- Taste: One thing that you taste

Complete this exercise by taking another deep breath.

Slow Down or Stop Whatever You Are Doing

When you slow down, you become more aware of your surroundings and fully see what you are observing. When we rush through the day, it can be difficult to notice much of anything.[26] So dial back the pace of your life a little, or a lot if needed. Sometimes life will force you to slow down when you least expect it.

Remember Being Present

Can you think of a time that you have already experienced when you were not distracted by anything? Reliving that moment in your mind can help you be present.

When you choose to be free of digital distractions, do breathing or mindfulness exercises, or intentionally slow down, there is a chance you may begin to feel things that are uncomfortable. Those are your true feelings. They could have been buried in distractions or the business of staying busy. They might not all be positive. But they are okay. If temporarily going offline is uncomfortable or exhilarating for you, grab a pen and paper and write down what you are feeling.

Journaling is another excellent method for reducing anxiety and can lead to powerful insights, which is why it's part of my daily informal mindfulness practice. And since you've got a pen in hand now, be sure to include three things, people, or life experiences every day that you are grateful for no matter how big or small.

Even if you have the attention span of a shoelace—as I used to—tuning into your senses using the tips listed above can help you become present and get more out of your efforts to connect with new people.

Further examples of how you can expand your own formal and informal mindfulness practice are explained in detail by Tracey Delfs in the Appendix. She taught me the difference between the two. Tracey is a good friend and mindfulness expert whom I met on Day 227 of the Talk2MorePeople Project. She kindly agreed to share her wisdom in this book. That's where you'll find the full thought-pie on the Meditator's Mindset. Enjoy.

THE TRAVELLER: BE ADVENTUROUS _____

Twenty years from now, you will be more disappointed
by the things you didn't do than by the ones you did.
—H. Jackson Brown

There is a reason that travel has been romanticized in Western society. That's because it's a wonderful thing to experience. Travel allows people to explore, discover, learn about other cultures, and be adventurous. It is educational and enjoyable, and it strips people of their biases. Thinking like a traveller can help bring more people into your life.

What Is the Traveller's Mindset?

The Traveller's Mindset means living life to the fullest while being your true, authentic self. It involves speaking your mind, doing what you want to do on your own terms while being independent, free, and adventurous. These are common feelings that many people report experiencing while travelling. But you don't need to live like Indiana Jones or James Bond to be adventurous.

The Traveller's Mindset means living life to the fullest while being your true, authentic self.

Simply experiencing life outside of your normal surroundings or circumstances can create these wonderful feelings and experiences. And the nice thing is that you can choose the environment you deposit yourself into.

Obstacles to the Traveller's Mindset

Thinking about social situations like a traveller will be easier for people who have travelled than for those who haven't. People who have never left their hometown, province, territory, state, or country may not have felt the many benefits of being adventurous, so it may seem like a vague concept.

Below are the main obstacles that you could face in attempts to embrace the Traveller's Mindset:

- No experience travelling, so an inability to relate
- No understanding of the benefits
- Worry that friends, family, and colleagues will judge your new, more open behaviour
- Belief that people in your city are extra unfriendly[27]
- Belief that faraway places are more fascinating than home
- Fear of the unknown

Benefits of the Traveller's Mindset

Speaking with fellow travellers, whether you encounter them on the road in their own country or elsewhere, reveals that they experience these common benefits:

- They feel less limited by inhibitions, which allows for more authenticity.
- They have a strong sense of independence and freedom.
- They learn so much about themselves.
- They are more open to new experiences.
- They are more likely to enjoy interacting with people who are different from themselves (race, religion, sexual identity, etc.).

- They feel more present, curious, spontaneous, adventurous, and adaptable.
- They attract like-minded people and feel more self-confident.
- They more easily and more often experience life-changing adventures.
- They increasingly feel open to saying yes to situations they would normally say no to.
- They turn into expert problem solvers.

You can bring this mindset home with you if you Talk2MorePeople because of the unpredictable opportunities and experiences you will bring into your life. These adventures will come to you through the people you meet. It's as if the people who you have not yet met hold the key to these benefits, so give yourself a chance to unlock that potential.

Travelling can open your mind and allow you to see the best in people, which creates transformational experiences. So how can you transform too?

Tips to Experience the Traveller's Mindset

You can build upon the curiosity you felt while travelling (in your own country or abroad) and allow yourself to be more explorative while at home. If you have yet to travel, play with the suggestions below just the same. While it might be difficult to think like a traveller while at home, you will notice that there is much to discover in previously familiar territory. Ultimately it's a choice to be adventurous.

- Go to events that you don't usually attend.
- Visit places that you've never been to.
- Explore markets for local food.
- Speak to people you normally pass by.
- Visit your local tourist trap and find out what the hype is all about.
- Spend the day out without any devices. Ask people for help getting information.
- Explore with a friend or family member who needs to get out more.
- Think or talk about what your life would be like if you were more adventurous.
- Reflect on a time in your life when you felt adventurous.

If you believe that local people can be as friendly and open as those who you've had adventures with while travelling, then guess what? You will begin to find these people and they will begin to find you. By embracing the Traveller's Mindset, you may even be able to wake up someone in a zombie state whose eyes are glued to a device.

Sure, the setting may be different. In your hometown, you likely won't be smashing pints in a youth hostel or a campground. You might not be visiting stunning museums and famous historical monuments. But there are plenty of opportunities to embrace this Traveller's Mindset while at home. My travel experience began way back in 1998 in Whistler, British Columbia, and the lessons I learned from that time and the travel career that followed continue to enrich my life to this day.

My Adventure

My formal education in Ontario, Canada, left me with a bachelor's degree in communication studies, and uncertainty about what to do next, So it seemed logical after university to hit the road. That was the beginning of my informal education.

At twenty-three years old, I sold my possessions, bought a plane ticket, and moved to British Columbia. First I visited my high school buddy Anthony DeLorenzo in Victoria. Then I "settled" in Whistler for work and adventure and easily found both. But I needed a place to stay. A week after arriving in Whistler, during a shift at a video store (it was the '90s), I met an English traveller, Jon Stromberg. A conversation was all it took. He kindly told me I could "kip on the couch at the flat." He invited me to join him and his friends at the Boot Pub (which sadly no longer exists), and I said, "Yes."

That was the first time I had met so many international travellers. There were accents that I'd never heard before and people with coloured hair, and everybody was friendly. That night it felt as if I had gone to school or played years of sports with these people, yet we'd only just met.

A new world had opened up for me—the world of travelling. When we got back to the four-bedroom flat in Creekside, there were sixteen travellers living there. The place was a cluttered, wild, ski-bum house. And despite the smell of winter gear and spilled beer, it was magical. It seemed like there was always a party going on. I stayed on the sofa or the floor for about a month.

Jon became a close friend. Instantly hooked on travelling, I moved to the UK on a working-holiday visa in 1999. Jon and I took a four-month backpacking trip to Eastern Europe as hobos. We travelled to fifteen European countries together at a time before the EU or the euro fully existed. We had to use different currencies in every country. It was the greatest and most random adventure of my life, and on that trip, Jon gave me the best gift that anyone has ever given to me. He taught me how to juggle.

Altogether, I travelled and worked abroad in a colourful spectrum of jobs for eight years. As far as career paths go, mine wound up and down hills, across rivers, deep into foreign lands, over mountains, and, at times, into dark places. The path that I chose was not paved.

On that trip, Jon gave me the best gift that anyone has ever given to me. He taught me how to juggle.

If people catch the travel bug, I caught the flu. While living in other countries, being open to meeting people—like my father was—introduced me to many life-changing experiences. Unknowingly, I was still studying communications by interacting with hundreds of people from all over the world.. Diverse jobs and conversations took me to diverse places: I worked in Japan, Uzbekistan, Brazil, England, Greece, and Ukraine and visited forty countries.

These travels had me glowing and growing as my desire to become immersed in other cultures and languages grew stronger and stronger. If you have an opportunity to live abroad, please go do it. The information gift exchanges you can have while travelling will shape and improve your life. But don't just take it from me. Ask anyone you know who has travelled, and they'll tell you to get out there.

There are far more benefits from living with the Traveller's Mindset than can be listed here. But my wish is that my international story will encourage you to consider how being adventurous could be good for you too. It might be exactly what you need, and it can definitely help you meet people.

It is not the strongest of the species that survives, nor the most intelligent. It is the one that is most adaptable to change.
—*Charles Darwin*

If you haven't yet, you will soon see that meeting new people is very unpredictable. I believe that is part of what makes it so magical, and I also understand that is part of the reason many people fear talking to strangers more than they fear a pack of rabid dogs. If you learn to be more adaptable during your interactions with people and in your life in general, the pressure to "get it right" will decrease and conversations will flow more smoothly.

The Juggler's Mindset is about being adaptable with whatever circumstances come your way.

The Juggler's Mindset is about being adaptable with whatever circumstances come your way. Jugglers need to be relaxed and to quickly adapt when things don't go as planned. As a juggler, I can tell you that this happens often! There are collisions, drops, audience interruptions, and changes to your routine that are completely unpredictable. Countless times I've wanted to spontaneously juggle for people (or myself) in public, but I didn't have juggling balls. Did that stop the show? Of course not. I picked up lemons at the grocery store, stones at the beach, or whatever objects I could find to manipulate in the air.

When you start to put the Talk2MorePeople process into practice, you will have more and more opportunities to explore and expand your ability to be adaptable, which is a valuable life skill.

Obstacles to the Juggler's Mindset

Adaptation is something we do every day, week, month, and year, as things change around or within us. But some people appear to be better than others at adapting. The common obstacles preventing you from being adaptable are worth reflecting upon:

- No interest in change/satisfaction with the status quo

- No understanding of the benefits

- A very structured personal or professional life, possibly influenced by family expectations

- Fear of the unknown

Benefits of the Juggler's Mindset

There have certainly been times in your life when everything was in flux and you had to respond to changes rapidly. So you may already know many of the benefits to being adaptable. Adaptable people:

- Are better equipped to deal with unexpected career or life changes

- Are more self-assured (knowing that they can handle anything)

- Enjoy problem solving

- Get to discover and use skills they did not know they had

- Are good mediators

- Can relax into any situation

- Are competent travellers

- Bounce back more quickly from adversity

How Did You Adapt When Everything Changed?

If you were anywhere on Earth in 2020, then the COVID-19 pandemic gave you a crash course on becoming more adaptable. How did your work experience change? How did you handle your kids suddenly being out of school? How did you manage your life when everything got turned upside down?

This is one recent example of a time when you had no choice but to be adaptable. Chances are, you were able to do it, even if it wasn't enjoyable. So, how did you manage in such times? Now, if you have to adapt to meeting people for your own good, you can. It is possible to meet people even when there are major changes in the world.

I met dozens of strangers while the world slowed down. Many people who tended to keep to themselves before became more open to meeting people in the pandemic. When people go through a life experience as dramatic as this together, they bond. Talk2MorePeople encounters happen more easily because people talk to one another about it, as they share the unique life experience.

"When are we going to finally be able to go outside again?"

"Yeah, I find these masks uncomfortable too."

"I can't wait for everything to get back to normal."

It is well documented that people who lack social connections are at risk for premature mortality.[28] Loneliness is a killer. Sometimes I could tell that a person was starving for human contact as they said hello while gingerly keeping the appropriate distance apart in public. Sometimes people would dive right into conversation. It seems to me that now it's easier than ever to meet strangers because people miss in-person interactions so much. You can test this out. While the pandemic changed how we experience in-person gatherings, we must not stop interacting face to face. It is more vital now than ever. You can use the unusual factors as talking points to get a conversation going. It is a unique, new opportunity to create more unexpected connections. Be the person who offers up that much-needed human connection. Be like a juggler and adapt.

Be the person who offers up that much-needed human connection.

Tips to Embrace the Juggler's Mindset

- Don't be afraid to drop the ball. Any adventure will have its ups and downs, so roll with them.
- Maintain a positive attitude, knowing that you are creating opportunities for connection.
- Continue learning and ask for feedback. Be more open to suggestions, offers, and ideas.
- Invite others to play with you.
- Put yourself in situations that aren't normal and familiar to you, but stay out of danger, because that's no fun.
- Experiment to see what happens.
- Notice times in your life when you have been adaptable before.

Learning to juggle is the greatest gift that I have ever received because of how many people it has brought into my life. The most practical lesson of my informal education, it has positively influenced much of what I do professionally as a facilitator and performer, and it eventually led me to join the circus.

The twenty-four-year-old version of myself could never have imagined that by galivanting around Europe like a hobo with another juggler I'd be learning skills to use for the rest of my life. But that's part of why travelling is so wonderful. It's the furthest thing from a classroom, yet you learn so very much about how to live. Travel guides you into the Juggler's Mindset. With all of the new stimulation that you encounter, you can't help but become more adaptable.

If you would like a little inspiration on how to use more of your imagination and creativity to connect with new people, why not visit the night circus? The night circus is a mysterious and sensational place where reality is bent and the unexpected unfolds before you.[29] Worlds of experience await those who dare step inside the tent, drop their judgment and inhibitions, and let the magic happen. This is no different from meeting new people.

Running Away with the Circus

In 2013 I moved from Toronto to Calgary. I needed a fresh start and was invited west by my supportive twin sister Andrea. Six months later, on an evening when I didn't feel like doing anything or seeing anyone, my close friend and roommate Rob suggested that we go out for beers. I resisted at first, but I am grateful for his persuasion on that evening. I couldn't possibly have known while in our apartment—and still in a bad mood—that I was about to meet a stranger who would positively impact my life.

We went to the local pub where we were regulars, called Bottlescrew Bill's.

Our waitress, named Ashley, was friendly and chatted a little with us while we drank our pints.

When we asked about her interests, Ashley mentioned, "I do performing work with hula hoops." This led me to comment, "Oh cool. I perform with glow-in-the-dark juggling balls." Then she floored me by saying, "Well then. You should audition for this cool circus in town!" "Hang on. What? There's a circus in Calgary?" I exclaimed, almost jumping out of my seat. "Yes, it's called Le Cirque de la Nuit and they are holding auditions soon. You should look them up."[30]

Do you know the feeling when you learn about something new that fits just perfectly into your life? That feeling of excited invigoration that you can feel in your chest? That feeling of being truly alive? I felt it! Meeting new people creates more opportunities for this to happen. Taking note of what I'd gained in our information gift exchange, I became giddy with excitement. You wouldn't have recognized the moody fellow who walked into the bar that night. He was gone.

I auditioned, and Cirque booked me to perform at their next big show, called Arniko. It took place in February 2014 in Calgary. My role in the show was to dance, juggle, and to let out a character. I was one of over twenty performers who—along with the production, decor, and design teams, volunteer co-ordination, and musical talent—co-created a fully immersive night-circus experience. It was sold out and over capacity. Most of the patrons were also dressed up. I'd spent more than two hours with a professional makeup artist. I had never been a part of an event like this before. It was a turning point in my performing career.

I literally ran away with the circus because I met and talked to a stranger.

That was the first of dozens of Cirque shows that I've now had the privilege to participate in. Learning about the circus has not only filled my soul with joy and given me an income doing work I love, it has also provided me with dozens of audiences to play with and entertain. Performers love to have audiences because we can feel how we touch people with our art through the reactions that we witness.

I am so grateful for the impact that that random conversation with Ashley had on me. It cost nothing more than a few moments of her time to share that information, yet it was so significant for me both personally and professionally. Now we have performed across Canada and delivered a performance for TEDxYYC. I literally ran away with the circus because I met and talked to a stranger.

What an incredible and unexpected gift. What gifts are waiting for you when you try on the Juggler's Mindset?

THE LOOKUP PROCESS FOR MEETING PEOPLE

In this section we will go through the LOOKUP Process for Meeting People. Each letter represents a different stage of the process. Keep the acronym LOOKUP in mind or just remember to look up from time to time to make connections, and this material will stick with you.

 Listen

 Overcome
Internal Obstacles

 Open a Dialogue
—Six Strategies

 Keep (the Conversation)
Going

 Uncomfortable?
How to Exit a Conversation

 Play and Improvise

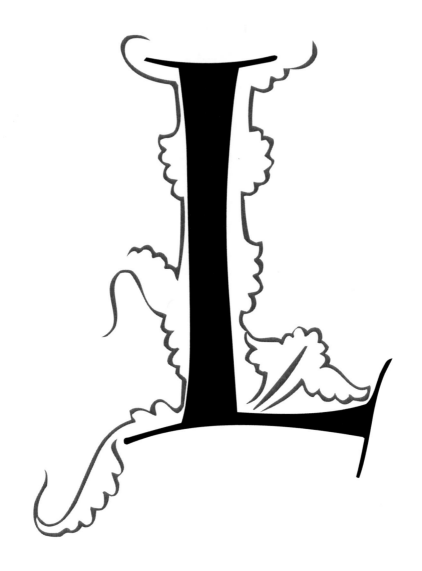

Listen

L: LISTEN

I always tell my colleagues to "listen to understand rather
than listen to respond." Because when you are thinking about
what you are going to say, you're not actually listening.
And you can tell when somebody is listening to you.
—Joelle
(a stranger from Day 332 of the Talk2MorePeople Project)

It's no secret that listening is an essential component of effective communication. But what is not so widely understood is how it is also an extremely accessible technique for connecting with new people.

Depending on your sources, there are anywhere between four and twelve types of listening, but these are the five most commonly referenced types:[31]

- Active/Attentive Listening—listener makes use of verbal and non-verbal cues to let the speaker know that they are solely focused on them and are deeply following along

- Appreciative Listening—for the pleasure of listening to sounds, music, words, or entertainment

- Comprehensive Listening—learning and remembering information

- Critical Listening—evaluating and analyzing what is being said

- Empathetic Listening—emotionally connecting with another person and showing them compassion

We'll return to active and empathetic listening later in the chapter when we look at some tips for being a good listener while a conversation is ongoing. But first let's consider a different kind of listening that is not listed here. I call it Talk2MorePeople Listening and it happens before your conversation with a stranger even begins.

Talk2MorePeople Listening is respectfully and intentionally overhearing what people are saying so that you can join a conversation.

Choosing to listen to conversations that you are surrounded by enables countless opportunities, experiences, and people to come into your life. If this is new to you, it might very well be uncomfortable. Starting to practise and eventually mastering this skill is an essential part of making new connections, and it can be used daily.

"But isn't eavesdropping considered rude?"

Eavesdropping is rude, yes. When you listen in to a conversation to effectively steal information without consent, that's a big no-no. Please don't do that.

Eavesdropping vs. Talk2MorePeople Listening

Talk2MorePeople Listening is different. It is listening for a good cause. It involves listening with the positive intention to meet a new person, learn something, or share knowledge. So if you approach Talk2MorePeople Listening with a positive intention you'll have a higher likelihood of it working out because of that positivity. If you don't, it very well might not. Unfortunately, there is no guarantee that even with the best intentions, a new connection will happen. Remain positive and do your best to expect positive results. Two examples of a positive intentions that you can use are:

"My intention is to be of service to someone in the world today."

"My intention is to be open to meeting a new person today."

Write your intention down, say it to yourself or say it out loud.

Even with a positive intention, though, it's best to be discreet. If you notice that the strangers are discussing a sensitive topic or if they appear upset or sad, give them their privacy by tuning out and leave them alone.

If someone does notice you listening to their discussion, be honest because you just got busted. But don't stress out about it. Simply confess. Say something along the lines of, "Oh, excuse me. I couldn't help but overhear (whatever you heard) and I'm interested in that." You may suddenly be invited into a conversation, possibly before you think you are ready. Remember, you are likely more capable of conversing than you think, just like learning to juggle.

Are you still uncomfortable about the idea of listening in to a conversation? Consider this. Our cell phones currently listen in to everything we say, most often without our consent. They eavesdrop to send data to big companies for profit. Have you noticed targeted ads on subjects that you were recently discussing (but didn't actively search for online)? At least you are not sitting there recording everything you hear and sending it off to a massive conglomerate for profit. Of course, your phone probably is, but that's a tough one to manage these days.

I challenge you to become more comfortable with Talk2MorePeople Listening and to do it with a positive intention. This type of listening works well as a starting point, because you don't need to approach anyone yet. For now, just listen to discover what you can hear.

You will be impressed with what you notice, hear, see, or learn by simply listening. So much can be gained as a silent observer, and this all takes place before you even attempt to interact with someone. I have heard people talk about the news and upcoming events. I have enjoyed listening to people laugh, tell jokes, and speak different languages. I have heard people discuss outdoor activities—which always interest me—and even share personal stories. You may already be aware of how certain keywords that you hear grab your attention, so build on that.

More than once I've heard new parents celebrate or complain about parenting. It is fairly common to overhear people speaking about how digital connection is making human face-to-face connection more difficult.

Take time to experiment with the following tips. You will be surprised by how easily you can relate to the things that you start to hear. This comes naturally to those who can become present. A previously unnoticed world of communication is constantly happening all around you. Once you practise the skills to join a discussion, you get to become a part of it.

In the coming chapters of this book, you will learn how to use what you have heard as your foot-in-the door to join a conversation. But not yet.

How to Respectfully Overhear Conversations

There are two parts to this: (1) respectfully listening and (2) overhearing conversations.

To respectfully listen, use your best judgment. If you hear something that makes you question, *Oh, yikes! Should I really be listening to this?* then you probably shouldn't. If it's your run-of-the-mill conversation, then it's probably fine. While I do suggest that you put effort into really listening to what you can hear as a technique for meeting people, I also recommend that you do so only with a positive intention: to make a new connection.

The tips below will go into how technically to overhear conversations. Please do so respectfully.

1. Digitally Disconnect

In order to use listening to make connections, you need to digitally disconnect for a while. This will likely be challenging or it may even seem impossible, depending on how attached you are to your technology. These devices and applications are designed to be addictive by the most advanced and wealthiest companies in the world.[32] So don't blame yourself if you find it difficult to put them down. The odds of being able to manage your time on your phone are stacked against you. Every time you receive a notification, you receive a little dose of dopamine. But that doesn't have to mean that you have no control.[33] Of course, you always have a choice to put it on silent, turn it off, or get that time vampire out of sight. Having the devices silent, off or best of all, in a different room makes it more possible to connect with people in person.

Experiment by leaving the house once a week (gasp) without your phone! If you survive that, work up to once a day. Or designate certain hours in a day when you don't look at the phone, such as the morning. If you do this, you will find that your ability to be present to social situations improves. Loosening the grip that your devices have on you is a very worthwhile and empowering exercise. What would your life look like if you were indistractable? For an excellent resource on digitally disconnecting, productivity, and mastering your time with tech, I highly recommend the national best-selling book *Indistractable* by Nir Eyal.

2. Use Selective Hearing (Point Your Hearing)

As of 2021, humans can do something that artificial intelligence cannot. This is "selective hearing" or "selective auditory attention." We can choose what to listen to and, in turn, what auditory stimulus to consciously allow into our brain. This developed as a survival mechanism when we were hunter-gatherers. It is our natural ability to focus on something while tuning other noise out.[34]

So in a busy café, restaurant, or grocery store, for example, you can choose to tune in to the music, the sounds of your thoughts, or another conversation. I find it's somewhat like a super power that most of us don't know we have. Give it a try. People are talking around us all the time, and it's your choice to respectfully, and with a positive intention, listen up to get involved. Use this human ability to connect with other humans.

3. Be a Detective and Practise Talk2MorePeople Listening

As you intentionally listen to conversations and the cacophony of ideas that are afloat in your surroundings, it is as if you are swimming in a pool of possibilities. And you have the opportunity to contribute to that pool by jumping in. At this stage, you don't have to. While learning this skill, take the pressure off yourself; you don't need to know how to approach someone until you've reviewed the entire process.

First, it's time for you to be a detective. Pay attention to one or more conversations that are happening around you. Investigate the specific words that are being said. Notice if the subject matter is related to something from your fantastic life experience or something that you are interested in.

Your knowledge about the subject matter becomes your *excuse* to join the conversation.

For example, you might overhear a discussion about a particular new type of tool, tech, or toy for a child that you recently purchased. You know features that haven't been mentioned yet. Or perhaps these strangers share your keen interest in travel or exotic cheeses. These topics catch your attention because the words sound familiar, stimulate thoughts and activate memories and bodies of knowledge in your mind. Once your outrageously powerful brain is stimulated, it will deliver you thoughts, ideas, and even words about the conversation that you are listening to. Often you will know that the thoughts, ideas, and words that pass through your mind at lightning speed are juicy and brilliant. Your knowledge about the subject matter becomes your *excuse* to join the conversation. In the section "Open a Dialogue," you will learn exactly how to use these ideas and words to start or join a conversation. But even if you don't muster up the courage to chime in this time, you are still practising Talk2MorePeople listening.

This type of listening happens naturally for many people. You pick up details about the aspects of life that you are already familiar with. I wouldn't suggest you interrupt a conversation about Greek mythology if you've never heard of Zeus. Unless, of course, you are keenly curious to learn. Your ears may perk up when you hear subjects discussed that you would like to learn more about, and this can help you join conversations as well.

Listening During a Conversation

I'm sure we can agree that fully listening to the person with whom you are speaking is important, right? When you show interest in others, they are more likely to be interested in what you have to say. Apparently not everybody knows this because you can see people half-listening by tapping away on a device while in conversation all the time. What tips should we—as listeners—explore to show that we are truly with the speaker?

1. Speak Less

Becoming a strong listener takes time and practice. It doesn't come naturally to most people, and it sure didn't for me. Also, not everybody bothers to try to improve this skill. You've got to practise to get good at it, like learning any circus skill. A simple way to improve your listening skills without much thought is to simply speak less during conversations.

Become curious about what is important to a person and consider how you might support them with your knowledge, connections, and resources.

2. Be of Service

Be there for the other person. Approach your interactions with humility. Ask yourself "How can I be of service?" rather than thinking of what you will get out of the conversation. This is a well-known practice that many successful people strive for. It works at networking events as well. Become curious about what is important to a person and consider how you might support them with your knowledge, connections, and resources. When an idea pops up, share it and watch the smile grow on their face.

3. Use Your Body Language

Only seven percent of human communication is through the spoken word. The remainder is through body language and tone of voice. Here are a few things to keep in mind:

- Smile naturally. Happiness tends to make most people happy.

- Make and maintain natural eye contact unless doing so goes against the cultural norm. You will stand out as caring and genuine by being vulnerable like this, and it helps you come across as non-threatening. But don't endlessly stare into their soul. Trust your own judgment. In "Why Meeting Another's Gaze Is So Powerful," Christian Jarrett tells us that three seconds is the average amount of time that works well for connecting with strangers.[35]

- You can also show them that you are interested in the discussion with your body positioning and posture. Face them directly. Ensure your feet are pointing in their direction; feet pointing away indicates you are keen to move along and out of the conversation. Lean in a little.

- Try mirroring. We naturally mirror people's speech and body movements when we are connecting with them. You can do this with the intention to deepen the connection. This is easy to mess up, and people can catch on, so be cautious. But more often than not, you will become aware of how you and the other person just do it automatically.

- Uncross your arms to offer open body language that says, "Yes, I'm here listening to you and everything's good."

4. Practise Active Listening

In active listening (also known as "attentive listening"), you more deeply connect with the speaker by showing how engaged you are in what is being said. The intention is to focus all mental energy on listening without getting distracted by anything else. While listening actively, the listener will use verbal and non-verbal cues to indicate that they are following along.

With some cultural differences, verbal cues may include positive reinforcement, remembering, questioning, reflection, clarification, and summarizing. Non-verbal cues include smiling, the use of eye contact, affirming posture, mirroring (as the last tip touched on), and avoiding distractions.[36] Don't look over their shoulder to see what is going on around them. That type of divided attention will get you less than favourable results because you will make the other person feel unimportant.

5. Practise Empathetic Listening

Empathetic listening involves emotionally connecting with another person and showing compassion for them. It is a very deep and personal form of listening where the listener offers support but not advice. If you are the listener, the focus is on the other person.

To improve your empathetic listening skills, try the following tips from the article "What Is Empathetic Listening?" by Jaya Ramchandani:

1. Create a safe space for the person/s who needs to talk.

2. Pay attention to body language. Use attentive posture, comfortable eye contact, and gestures, expressions, and intensity that match the speaker's.

3. Use thoughtful, open-ended, empathic questions to invite deeper thought and consideration: "What were you feeling when that happened?"

4. Remind yourself that respectful empathetic listening is a *gift* you may give, and it doesn't mean "I agree with you."

5. When the speaker pauses, you can briefly summarize what you heard in your own words, without providing solutions (this is the hardest part). When you need to say something: introject, don't interrupt.[37]

It is essential to be sensitive to the speaker and to put their needs first. To demonstrate our empathy, we can use these verbal and non-verbal cues to encourage openness.

A fundamental first step to connecting with new people, Talk2MorePeople listening will allow you to practise listening before approaching anyone. It is a safe way to start out. Once the conversation begins, active and empathetic listening—as well as the other tips I've offered above—will take you the rest of the way.

Thank your listening skills for guiding you to respectfully overhear a discussion that you can join. Even if you have not tried this yet, now you know how to. Next, let's find out how to overcome common internal obstacles we face when approaching new people.

Listen

 Overcome
Internal Obstacles

 Open a Dialogue
—Six Strategies

 Keep (the Conversation)
Going

 Uncomfortable?
How to Exit a Conversation

 Play and Improvise

Overcome
Internal Obstacles

O: OVERCOME INTERNAL OBSTACLES

Life begins at the end of your comfort zone.
—*Neale Donald Walsch*

People experience many different internal obstacles when attempting something new. Remaining in the same pattern of behaviour can feel comfortable and safe, but this can be very limiting. Meeting new people is a big challenge. There is no denying that. Here we will explore the most common internal challenges people face when meeting new people and offer a number of tips to overcome them.

What you see in the world is largely a result of your expectations. On the one hand, this is a frustrating thought because it can mean that, with a negative attitude, you will only be able to see negative people, experiences, and bad opportunities. If you believe that it's impossible to meet people, you will only see people with their heads down in their technology, closed to the world and appearing closed to you. But on the other hand, the positive opposite is also true.

I think this is an exciting concept. As individuals, we in a sense have an opportunity to shape our reality by being disciplined with our thoughts.

Before attempting to jump into a conversation with someone you've never met before, it is a good exercise to explore what your experience in meeting strangers has been so far.

Reflections, Part One

Reflecting on any learning process deepens the learning.[38] Reflect on your current attitude towards meeting new people. This can help you identify your opportunities for growth. Consider the questions below.

Questions to Explore	Your Answers
What have you heard while Talk2MorePeople listening?	
What are your best hopes from learning to meet people?	
What has been working for you?	
With the skills you have now, how might it be possible to meet new people?	

You might be concerned about what another person is thinking, and you may have negative internal chatter going on at the same time. That can be distracting and stressful, but you can get past it by really thinking about the questions above. In doing so, you may notice that talking to strangers is not entirely new to you after all. Below are common excuses people give themselves and others for why they can't meet people, along with challenges to those excuses.

Common Obstacles for Meeting People and How to Get Over Them

"I Am Not an Extrovert."

Good to know. But this doesn't mean that you can't learn how to meet people. I used to be highly introverted as well. There is nothing wrong with being introverted; however, you can benefit from practising skills that extroverts enjoy naturally. Think of it as a new skill, not as a personality swap.

Introversion can be a great strength. Introverts are often the best listeners in the room. Being able to listen is essential when making new connections, so this can give you a head start.

"I Don't Feel Comfortable Sharing My Personal Information."

Remain anonymous. You don't need to share your name to help someone out or to learn from them. You only need to be involved in the discussion. Give and take what is comfortable for you, and expand upon it in time.

Introversion can be a great strength. Introverts are often the best listeners in the room.

"I Don't Have Time for This."

Incorrect. Meeting strangers takes more intention than time. It can happen in seconds. Very often, these encounters happen in your spare time or between appointments. If you keep a present and curious mindset, you will notice that you already have the time to allow new people into your life.

"I Don't Have Anything Useful to Share."

Yes, you do. You don't need to carry around an *Encyclopedia Britannica* when meeting people to share information, although it's a heck of a resource. After all, those books are heavy. Instead, draw from your own unique life experience to come up with information to exchange. The next time you think that you have nothing to talk about with someone, consider that you've lived a full life until now, no matter how wild, free, and creative or seemingly programmed, mundane, and straightforward. In your unique life experience, there are stories to share, experiences to expand upon, and knowledge to pass on.

What activities within or outside of your work make you feel positive and give you energy? What lights you up? Observe the subjects that you bring up in conversation with friends, and use them in conversation with someone who you don't yet know. Also, many people greatly enjoy speaking about themselves, so it may be easier than you think.

"It's Impossible to Meet People During a Pandemic."

No, it's not. I have met several lovely people during the pandemic, even once while in quarantine.[39] You can meet people in the strangest places. I met Sam as he appeared outside the balcony while suspended from a cable. He was washing the windows, so we had a conversation outside. While some people completely withdraw due to health restrictions, others allow themselves to still maintain communication with people but adapt to how it happens. That's an example of the Juggler's Mindset at work. To connect like an ace, do it face to face. But at times when that's not possible, I acknowledge that digital tools can be a big help to connect with people, so make use of them.

My friend Stephen shared with me what his organization in the UK is doing to maintain connection for their individuals: "As a way to fill the gap of the office coffee break chat, colleagues have started having virtual coffee breaks. This happens during working hours. They are organized on a fortnightly basis so you can catch up with people that you would have bumped into at the office or at a meeting. It's a great way to remain connected to others."

How brilliant is that?

"I'm Just Not a People-Person."

No problem. You don't have to be a people-person to meet people, but it helps. You do, however, need to be open to the possibility that meeting strangers could be good for you. Perhaps you've simply not yet noticed the wonderful contributions that other people, including strangers, have made to your life. It's easy to overlook the fact that every friend or lover we've ever had was once a stranger.

One reason people are afraid to meet strangers is the inherited or programmed fear that difference is dangerous. First of all, difference is not dangerous, and neither is diversity. They are beautiful! Secondly, people are not so different. And apart from occasional societal exceptions, we are far less threatening than we have grown up to believe. To get past this fear, we need to celebrate our diversity and share with others how similar we are as humans. We can achieve this by talking to one another.

Have you ever started speaking to someone at an event or party only to learn that you had personal contacts in common? Perhaps you found out that you worked in the same industry or had similar interests. Maybe you learned that you travelled to the same country or even went to the same school. Perhaps the conversation led you to the surprising discovery that you each had adorable yet needy little dogs. Somehow, you stumbled across a topic to discuss where you shared common ground. And once that was established, the conversation flowed naturally.

We need to celebrate our diversity and share with others how similar we are as humans. We can achieve this by talking to one another.

In your day-to-day experience, do you see familiar equipment or something that indicates a person likes a certain sport or hobby? You could say "Excuse me, I like your motorcycle." or comment, "Those acrylics look stunning." Neither of you has to be a people-person to strike up a conversation. But you both have to be open to it happening.

"I Don't Want to Offend Anyone."

Ah yes, of course. You are so polite. You must be Canadian. As a child, my mother used to always say, "It's the squeaky wheel that gets the grease." And my father had no concern about offending people with his thoughts. It took me years to learn that it was okay that what I had to say might not be liked or gain everyone's approval. It's a simple fact that when you use your voice, sometimes people will get offended. Don't let this stop you from making connections. Maybe there is even a part of you that would love to speak up more often, to share your thoughts. Why not dare to give that voice power and see what happens? Of course, even while using your voice, you still want to be respectful and careful not to do anything that intentionally makes someone uncomfortable, because that would be unwise, uncool, and unacceptable.

"I'm Too Awkward."

It's okay to be awkward. That's part of what makes you unique. Your awkwardness could be exactly the kind of endearing quality that a person really likes. Besides, awkwardness is authentic, and authenticity leads to connection. By being your authentic self, you will stumble upon more of yourself in the world (in the form of another person). But you'll never know this if you never speak up. And everybody is awkward in at least one area of their life. Remember, we are not all *that* different. The growth and rewards from putting effort into meeting new people will overpower your awkwardness.

"I Don't Know How to Make Small Talk."

So make big talk. Corinne, whom I met on a train on Day 107 of the Talk2MorePeople Project, told me this is an excuse she hears often. In response, she says, "If you don't make small talk, then don't bother trying to make small talk. Get into a real conversation if that's easier for you." More details on how to do that will be covered in the chapter "Keep (the Conversation) Going."

"I Don't Want to Interrupt/Bother Them."

Shift your perspective. Trust me when I say, in my experience of having intentionally met over three thousand people outside of my work, you are doing people a favour when you initiate a conversation with them. You provide them with a break in what might be a very monotonous, routine day. When you interrupt by asking a question, for example, it can be a pleasant surprise for that person. You create a human interaction that could lead to an opportunity or possibility of fun for them as well. Shift your perspective from feeling like you are interrupting to feeling like you are being of service.

"I Can't Think on My Feet/I Don't Feel Ready Yet."

So take a seat. There are several ways to address this internal obstacle. Ease into this by first writing down the thoughts and questions that are coming to you before saying anything out loud to a stranger. You can also let a supportive friend, partner, or colleague know the thoughts that you are having and what you plan to say when you are ready. But choose this person wisely. If they are genuinely supportive of your growth, then they will be happy for you. You can expect positive and helpful feedback. If the person you are with is closed-minded, then don't share your thoughts with them. They will only discourage you and—from their fear-based perspective—convince you that it's not worth the risk of rejection, and they could tell you to mind your own business. Let them have their views on meeting people, but don't let their views block your growth, openness, and development.

Another form of super-safe training is practising by asking a salesperson a question. Try this anywhere you have a transaction with someone, such as in a café, at the grocery store, in a doctor's waiting room, in line at the cafeteria, or at the post office. This is excellent practice and can also lead to excellent conversations. As they are at work, and you are the customer, they must answer you. The risk of rejection shrinks to a tiny fraction. It's okay if you need to try several times before reaching out to a completely random person. Just take the first step and start wherever you are now.

Finally, keep in mind that, as the initiator going out to intentionally meet someone, you're in a position of relative control. Starting a dialogue, you are in control of that which you can't control, because you never know how the chat will go. Does this sound enjoyable or terrifying? Can you let go of control for your own good? Allowing yourself to be spontaneous and open to whatever happens can be empowering, and improvising is a skill you can learn. More on that is coming up in the "Play and Improvise" chapter.

"I Can't Handle Rejection."

Nobody likes rejection, but everybody can handle it. It just might not be enjoyable. Rejection happens a lot less often than anticipated, and when it does, it isn't a big deal because these encounters are low-stakes. We have a tendency to make it a big deal in our head, but it's not.

T2MP Day 229

Today I had a bizarre experience while writing in The Roasterie coffee shop in Calgary. I overheard someone say exactly the same words I was writing at the very moment I was putting them down on paper. And then it happened again, with a different group of people. The first matching word was "sleeping"; the second phrase was "thinking about."

So I used this unique and what I consider to be bizarre phenomenon as my excuse to say hello with hopes of starting a conversation.

But I was boldly rejected! The first two people with whom I exchanged only three sentences just started talking amongst themselves again as if I wasn't even there. It was almost comical, but I didn't find it funny at the time. In my second attempt, the other two fellows at the coffee bar were speaking to the barista. One man acknowledged me and we spoke briefly before he suddenly turned away from me and back to his original conversation. I was more surprised than anything because it's so rare to be turned down for a chat, never mind twice in the same day. And that's okay.

Although I've met lifelong friends in this coffee shop—including my friend Charlotte—and I still consider it a great place to meet people, it wasn't happening today. I can't expect to have a successful conversation with every person I approach. Rejection will happen but not as often as we worry it will, in my experience. The first time I got rejected by someone I approached on this project was on Day 50.

Meeting strangers is very low-stakes. And at the end of the day, what does it really matter? These people were not offended that I tried to talk to them; they just wanted to keep to themselves. And after all, I may never see them again. It could be a source of concern if they were colleagues or someone I had to see every day. But they are strangers. I'll just meet people later today somewhere else.

Besides, we can look at rejection as progress. If I had not even tried to talk to these people today, perhaps I wouldn't have fulfilled my daily obligation to do so.

Although today's encounter surprised me, it didn't discourage me. Don't let it discourage you either.

"How Could Meeting a Stranger Positively Impact My Life? Why Should I Bother?"

Because people are awesome! Through human connection, we have the power to shape our lives. These connections lead to opportunities to grow and make a greater contribution to this world. We see a reflection of ourselves in society. So if you don't like what or who you see out there, you likely need to change some characteristics about yourself. With gritted teeth and clenched fists, I saw a reflection of myself that I didn't like and eventually (but not without a fight) submitted that I needed to change. The good news is that you don't need to rely on other people—whose actions you have no control over—to improve your situation.

Now that I've made personal changes, the world looks much better and the people I meet in the world look better too. Happiness is an inside job. It is, after all, impossible to change anyone else; each of us is responsible for our own happiness alone.

Why not explore what happens if you decide to not let limiting thoughts stop you from meeting people anymore? Despite your fear, you can choose to keep developing this skill and you will be rewarded for your efforts.

So now I see the good in everyone despite my internal obstacles. I see the beautiful, pure person/being who is in front of me, no matter what they are presenting (whether positive or negative) to me in the "real" world. It takes practice, but it can be done. It is a choice.

Reflections, Part Two

Let's take a moment to reflect more on the positive: What has been working in conversation attempts in the past? What are your strengths? Add your answers below.

Questions to Explore	Your Answers
Suppose that you learned how to meet people. What would that do for your life?	
On a scale from 10 to 1, how open are you to meeting strangers now? (10 being fully open)	
How did you get this far already? (no matter where you are on the scale)	
When have you already had a positive experience meeting a stranger?	

Encouragement to Overcome Internal Obstacles

We all have obstacles. Above, you have seen ideas to help you get past the typical obstacles to meeting strangers. It is easy to spend time and energy on why we can't do something, but it's also important to consider why we can and want to do it.

Beyond getting past your obstacles and bringing more adventure, mindfulness, new ideas, people, and play into your life, meeting new people also creates community and helps others.

Remember, people will often thank you for starting a dialogue with them. With practice and experience, you will hear strangers responding positively to you with comments like these:

- "Thank you for speaking with me. You made my day."
- "It was wonderful to meet you."
- "Thank you for letting me know about that."
- "People just don't talk to each other nowadays, and I appreciate you coming up to me."
- "Can we keep in contact?"
- "I needed to hear this today. Thank you."
- "Do you have a card?"
- "Could I introduce you to someone I know?"
- "May I tell you about an upcoming event that you should attend?"
- "What you were just speaking about makes me think of..."

The list of kind words from a stranger that will massage your ears goes on and on. All you have to do is start the interaction. Learning how to connect with other people is one way that you can create positive change in the world.

The person you are about to approach could positively transform your life in ways that you can't even begin to imagine.

The person you are about to approach could positively transform your life in ways that you can't even begin to imagine. There may be something within you that could positively change their life as well. Such transformation happens when your world of life experience collides with theirs.

When you act on these tips, eventually you will be astounded to notice that you've just had an enjoyable conversation with someone who you've only just met. You may share things that you haven't yet shared with a close friend or a partner. There is unique freedom in the anonymity of conversation with strangers that can allow for full authenticity in a very short period of time. For a few of us, this might be the first time in a long time that we've really been "real" to ourselves or another person. Celebrate the powerful insights that can positively affect a person. The stakes are irrelevant and high at the same time as your interaction may last just seconds or lead to a lifetime relationship. So relax into it. Here we go. Let's open a dialogue.

Listen

 Overcome
Internal Obstacles

 Open a Dialogue
—Six Strategies

 Keep (the Conversation)
Going

 Uncomfortable?
How to Exit a Conversation

 Play and Improvise

Open A Dialogue
—Six Strategies

O: OPEN A DIALOGUE: SIX STRATEGIES_____

I can tell you from experience, the effect you have on others
is the most valuable currency there is.
—*Jim Carrey*

Now that you have honed your Talk2MorePeople listening skills and overcome internal obstacles, it's time to open a dialogue. In this section are six of the strategies that I used to intentionally meet more than 550 people during the year-long Talk2MorePeople Project. These strategies have multiple angles, so you can use what you are most comfortable with. Remember, the desired outcome from approaching a stranger is to have an information gift exchange. As a result of your interaction, either you learn something from them or they learn from you. So where do you begin?

Questions

You can begin with a question. The moment when you approach a stranger and ask a question is so meaningful for several reasons:

- You are courageously making an offer to make a new connection.

- You are being vulnerable, which enables others to be vulnerable as well.[40]

- You are generously creating a moment of possibility when anything can happen.

- You are instigating an information gift exchange.

- It is astonishing what a question can lead to, but you never know if you don't ask.

Making use of questions to connect with people is something that many people do quite naturally.

"But what questions should I ask?" Now, that's a great question!

STRATEGY ONE: *How to Open with a Question*
Keep It Simple

Truthfully, you don't need a groundbreaking and stimulating question, so take that pressure off yourself. All you are looking for is an *excuse* to get into a conversation with someone, so a simple question will work very well. There's no need to get metaphysical just yet.

Take Cues from Your Surroundings

Look up and be curious. Use the Child's Mindset. While observing your surroundings, what visual cues stand out to you? What do you like about what you see? By noticing unusual objects that stand out to you, questions about the current situation will come to mind. Maybe a stranger nearby is curious about the same thing that you are or has the answers you're looking for.

You might ask, for example, "Excuse me, do you know what type of car that is?" Or say "Hi there. Have you noticed the huge flock of birds circling that building?" Or you could comment when you see an unexpectedly large group of people in matching uniforms, "Wow, that sure looks like a marching band, doesn't it?"

Each of those questions is an example of a technique called "triangulation," described by author Kio Stark. I recommend her book, *When Strangers Meet: How People You Don't Know Can Transform You*. In it she states, "Interactions between strangers increase when there is something to talk about, something to make an observation about, a third thing to close the triangle between the two people who don't know each other."[41] Look up and find an object or situation to remark on, and comment or question out loud about it.

Here are questions that could arise in a public establishment:

Your Thoughts	Turned into a Question
I wonder where this art comes from.	Do you know where this piece of art is from?
This room reminds me of something.	Does this room also make you think of the Victorian era?
Something strange is currently going on outside.	What's going on over there?
What a cool building.	Don't you just love this architecture?

Take cues from your surroundings to play with triangulation and kick off conversations.

Get Inspiration from the Person You'd Like to Talk To
"Wow! What's that?"

Allow your astonishment to guide you. Something the stranger is doing, saying, wearing, or holding could be the spark of inspiration you need. By being present, curious, and spontaneous, you will notice more of everything that happens around you.

At a café I saw a young couple sitting at a table and the woman had a small branch in her hand. Curious about it, I got up and started walking in their direction. It was only when I was on my way to the table that I discovered what I was going to ask. With a smile on my face, I said, "I'm sorry to interrupt you, but may I ask you a quick question? Why do you have this branch with you?" Anne happily replied, "I was on my way to meet a guy and this just fell right at my feet. So I picked it up. Listen to the cool sound it makes on the table. And smell the pine needles!" She held it up to my face. "I'm going to add it to my altar at home."

"Oh, that's great," I replied as we both laughed. "Thank you. Have a nice evening." This left me feeling positive because I love meeting new people and it satisfied my curiosity. The man she was sitting with, Taylor, seemed positive as well. The branch was the *excuse* that I needed to approach, and it worked. Can you see how this was also an example of triangulation?

Use this sentence or a variation of it to ask anyone anything anytime: "Excuse me. May I ask you a quick question?" And then follow up with your question.

Be Prepared with a Few Backup Questions
The most natural and authentic questions will be your own. But if you need assistance to get started, try one of these when it fits the situation:

- "What is the best activity to do nearby?"
- "How did you find out about this event?"
- "How long has this restaurant/café/bar/studio/vintage store been here?"
- "Do you know where the post office/pharmacy/grocery store/theatre/museum is?"

If you've ever studied another language, these questions may look familiar. They are simple questions to get your basic needs met. If you have travelled, you have likely asked a number of these. Keep the Traveller's Mindset of being adventerous to ask them while at home too.

For a little more fun, play with these:

- "I'm doing a personal survey. May I ask what the latest book was that you read/movie that you watched?"
- "If I was challenged to meet a new person today, what do you think would be a good question to ask?"
- "If you had a chance to share a message with the world, what would that be?"

Make Use of General Questions

You don't want to get too personal to start with, so use the examples above or your ideas. If the other person steers the conversation in a more personal direction, then it will be up to you if you want to engage in it.

Questions will take you places. Allow them to do so. Explore your curiosity as a method of coming up with questions to ask people, and dare to ask them. Yes, it takes courage to do so. But isn't building human connection worth it? Not only will you connect with people you otherwise wouldn't have met, you will also learn much more about your community and the world. You will be happy that you did.

Compliments

T2MP Day 314

While at the Door exhibit, I met Karen Jacobs and Doug Wong. They were both doing photography of the Glow Light Festival in downtown Calgary and I complimented Karen on her awesome glasses. She told me, "That's actually how I met Doug seven years ago. He liked the red glasses I was wearing at the time."

This reminds me of how important genuine compliments are for breaking the ice and creating conversations with random people.

Give it a go! The next time you see something that you think you could compliment someone on, go ahead and do it. You will probably be pleasantly surprised how easily you can engage with that person, and you never know what it could lead to.

Our visit was brief as they were moving on to another exhibit, but I'm thrilled to have met a couple of friends who had also met because of a compliment.

Why do we love being complimented?

There are psychological benefits for both the giver and the receiver of the compliment. According to the article "The Art of the Compliment" from *Psychology Today*, by Hara Estroff Marano, "Oxytocin is released when giving compliments so it stands to reason that the more compliments you give, the better you feel."[42] By the way, in case you haven't heard it yet today, you are a fantastic person on a wonderful adventure! I know this because you are exploring how to meet people, and that's a noble cause. Now give yourself a pat on the back. Well done.

Positive interactions between complete strangers happen naturally all the time when someone offers a genuine compliment. When you muster up self-confidence along with a good intention to express something positive to another person, you are truly giving them a gift. You are celebrating something that you appreciate and courageously letting them know about it. This can lift spirits and build connections.

You may be thinking, *How do certain people give compliments that get a warm response, while others are told to get lost?* There are two important factors: the level of authenticity and what's being complimented. Complimenting someone can be challenging, but don't fret. Just like juggling, we have to drop the ball from time to time. It is a necessary part of learning.

Soon I'll also share a story of a woman who is an expert at inviting compliments along with tips on how you can do this too.

STRATEGY TWO: *How to Give a Genuine Compliment*
Be Authentic

The importance of authenticity can't be overstated when we meet strangers. To be authentic, smile, make eye contact and respectfully ask the person what's on your mind when it occurs to you. By doing so, you connect with your true self, and the people with whom you interact will feel that. Remember that being spontaneous is one way to be authentic.

One such time, while entering a café in my city, I saw a person wearing fun, bright athletic tights. I spontaneously said, "Those are great tights!" There was no time between my observation and my comment. Because of this, I was introduced to a free worldwide fitness movement called the November Project.[43] The idea of working out at 6:13 a.m. outside sounded awful, but the hugs and high-fives were right up my alley. That day I met Tammara and Pete, the Calgary co-leads at the time, and I joked around with Brogan Graham, the co-founder of the November Project, who happened to be in town.

The next morning I participated in my first of dozens of free workouts. By participating in their workouts twice a week, not only did I improve my fitness, but I was also introduced to a new community of people in my city. They all challenged me to #justshowup and I did. Giving that authentic, spontaneous compliment changed my life. To find this community, check out November-Project.com to see if there's a chapter near you.

Avoid Complimenting a Person's Body

As a general rule, it's best not to compliment people on their bodies. It can be risky, annoying, and even disrespectful to comment on physical appearance.

If you see a beautiful person and have the instinct to tell them that, this is the one time when I would ask you not to spontaneously blurt it out. Keep it to yourself. There is a good chance they have already heard an unsolicited comment several times that day. So it will be experienced as a nuisance rather than received as a genuine compliment, no matter how good your intentions may be.

In most circumstances, you can compliment people on clothing items you genuinely appreciate. It is best to be specific about what you like:

- "Hey. Nice shirt."
- "I love your cool shoes."
- "Excuse me. I just had to tell you, that's a great sweater."

Please never use statements like "You look sexy." This is sexual harassment, which is completely unacceptable.

Compliment a Person's Hobby or Tastes

You can offer a comment to someone on an activity they are doing or are about to do. By commenting on a hobby that you are familiar with, it will be easier to speak with the person because you already have something to share and contribute. Here are some examples:

- "Oh, I love that book. Are you enjoying it?"
- "How long have you been into fishing?"
- "What kind of camera are you shooting with?"
- "What do you love most about acrobatic yoga?"

Compliment Character Traits

Far too often people are complimented on appearances, so if you can pick up on a character trait that you are observing, and use that as your compliment, it can work very well to break the ice. For example, "I just wanted to let you know that I really appreciate how kindly you spoke to that person" or "You seem to have a great sense of humour." If you can feel or see energy, you could authentically offer, "I recognize that you have great energy, and I just wanted to let you know that." If you can get the person to compliment themselves during your chat, the discussion will likely go very positively.

Make compliments to create connection, but don't unreasonably expect perfection.

Read the Signs

You will be able to tell based on their body language if the compliment is welcome or not. Respond accordingly. If they welcome a conversation, engage in it and enjoy. If they show closed body language—for example, they cross their arms, avoid eye contact, blatantly ignore or turn away from you—please leave them alone and go meet somebody else. Make compliments to create connection, but don't unreasonably expect perfection.

This won't work every time and that's normal. The truth is, no matter how kind and sincere your words are, there will always be a chance that people won't speak with you. At times, you might even offend someone, although it's extremely rare if you are not rude. Of course, this is something to steer clear of, but don't let that concern stop you from making new, wonderful connections with people that improve your well-being. Read the signs that people give you and respond accordingly.

Consider Your Compliment

If you are not yet ready to speak compliments out loud to another person, take mental or written notes of the things that you appreciate when looking at a person. Consider how they could be used as a genuine compliment to open a dialogue. Next, share it with whomever is nearby—a supportive friend, family member, colleague, or partner. For a real adventure, share it with a stranger. Discuss your observations to see if it could be an appropriate compliment and be open to their support or criticism. If nobody is around, write it down.

At the very least, get that compliment out of your head and into words even though it's not given directly to the individual whom you noticed. This is great practice, so keep at it. You are almost there. You are just about ready to bring a new person into your life.

Juggle the Conversation into an Information Gift Exchange

Here we go! Who knows what will come from your compliment, until you offer it? Play with what shows up to see if you can offer value or if you can learn something from the other person.

Here are the reasons why compliments often lead to deeper conversations:

- First of all, being complimented generally feels good, so it may encourage the recipient to lower their guard and open up.

- Secondly, sometimes there is a personal story behind the object you complimented.

A stranger can easily launch into the story of how that article of clothing or item came into their life. To your surprise, they might tell you quite a lot when asked about it because many people like to share their story. If they do go into a personal story with you—a complete stranger—you are in, so juggle that conversation and adapt with what comes up. They are comfortable with you.

Watch for Peacocks

If you keep an eye out for people who wear vibrant wardrobe items, you can feel more confident approaching because they likely want to interact with people. Often (but not always), they want to tell their story and are keen to meet people themselves.

When I wear my twenty-inch-tall hat outside, I expect to hear, "Great hat," and I'm happy to speak with anyone who positively heckles me. Wearing something flashy or eccentric is known as "peacocking."

People who strut their stuff often have more self-confidence than your average Jane or Joe and won't be surprised that you've approached them because it happens all the time. How might you spruce up your wardrobe to get people to come up to you? Below you can see how Ivan's cane helped me meet him.

T2MP Day 109

Following the suggestion from the Pie Cloud staff, I went to check out Slide the City. On my way through Riley Park, I thought to myself, I wonder who this suggestion is leading me to. Less than a minute later, I met Ivan and we talked.

I complimented him on a beautifully handcrafted walking stick that he had carved. It was elaborate and had an owl on it. He uses this because of recent knee surgery.

We spoke in the park for roughly thirty minutes about several things. Ivan commented, "People need people. We are social beings." He told me that his unique walking stick allows him to meet new people often, which he enjoys.

He also kindly invited me to visit his place to see more art and have another good conversation. I will take him up on this. (And I did.)

If your fear about meeting people is, "I don't know what to say," then follow Ivan's example. Make the stranger say something to you first. Invite a compliment.

Just as you are learning to appreciate things that you notice about people, you can be playful and use something to bring people to you. This might be a unique wardrobe piece, such as a pair of retro boots, a jacket made of mirrors, a bold belt, a really bright dress, or stylish glasses (if you want to go all in). Perhaps one day you'll decide to experiment with face paint or use another creative form of self-expression.

When you boldly use yourself as a canvas, it stimulates other people's curiosity and, as long as your outfit is in good taste, the compliments will begin to flood in. Tattoos draw attention as well. People are curious, and they are also nosy. It is difficult for certain people to walk past something that is so different without saying anything. They simply have to ask. This creates opportunities for you to have conversations with strangers. It requires a different type of self-confidence than you need when approaching people yourself, and you will hear people tell you that.

I estimate that at least eleven times as many people will notice you than will approach you, though it depends on your choice of attire. Be prepared for occasional strange looks, but don't be discouraged. It is courageous to intentionally stand out in public in a world of mediocrity, and you could make someone's day.

People are often peacocking at special events as well as nightclubs, but you can choose to do it anytime. Pick a day. How about Tuesday?

Mollie Kaye in Victoria, British Columbia, has an initiative called Turned-Out Tuesdays. Look for her on Instagram. While wearing vintage clothes to promote a friend's event, she had many people approach her. They offered compliments on her outfit that often led to deeper conversations. The experience was so profound for Mollie that she decided to dress up in vintage wear every Tuesday for a year. Here's what she has to say about it:

> *The way I think of my "strategy" is this: When I get turned out in a way that I think is snazzy, my overall sense of myself and my worthiness increases. Then, if it's comment-worthy (fancy hat, bright colour, bold pattern, sparkly pin, or overall historical effect), I know I'm a "happening" and I am ready to be engaged instead of looked over. Something about this makes me more inclined to be the giver of compliments. I think I am more often the person who makes the first move, saying, "Hey! I like the way your shoes match your snazzy jacket!" And then they say thanks and are all, "Wow, look at you! Love it!" I would say it's like when I put effort into my presentation, I have pre-energized myself with the motivation to "elect to connect."*

We met in person two months into her journey and she reported that her life was already transformed because of the people she had met.

When people ask Mollie why she is all dressed up, she responds, "I do this every Tuesday, so that I get to have conversations with people I otherwise would never get to meet." She collects compliments by putting on a vibrant outfit and a persona, but she doesn't do it for her ego. Mollie does it to increase the human connection.

STRATEGY THREE: *How to Invite a Compliment*
Keep It Simple
You don't need to wear a full flashy outfit to attract attention. A funky tie, amazing but not matching colourful socks (one of my favourite things to wear), a unique hat, or bright broach will all do the trick.

Be True to Yourself
Use something that is aligned with your values and personality. To begin with, you can expect to be uncomfortable going in public looking like a conversation magnet. I still do at times, even though I perform in a circus and love audiences. But if you are true to yourself with whatever that alteration is, you will have no trouble thinking of what to say when people approach.

Share Your Story

Everybody has a story to tell. When you invite a compliment, you create an opportunity for you to share yours. Use it. We can all take a tip from Mollie and "elect to connect" by being a little more snazzy than normal in public.

Juggle the Conversation into an Information Gift Exchange

Take what comments and compliments are offered to you and toss them around a little. You've taken the risk to be vulnerable and open by standing out. Now it's your job to enjoy the conversation that just landed in your lap. Play with this opportunity and enjoy what happens.

Help

Help in the broadest sense is in fact one of the most important
currencies that flow between members of society.
Because help is one of the main ways of expressing love and other
caring emotions that humans express.
—Edgar H. Schein

You still may not feel ready to start a conversation with a stranger. It is common to feel limited, uncomfortable, self-conscious, unconfident, insecure, intimidated, or incompetent when this is new. But using help to say hi can replace these fears. When an opportunity to be helpful arises, there is rarely time for thought, analysis, or self-doubt.

When you offer help, you create opportunities to connect, and sometimes it will happen without you even realizing you are doing it. Selfishly, it will also make you feel great. Studies have shown that when people help each other out, the person offering the help also feels better.[44]

It can be something as simple as giving directions or helping a person buy a bus ticket. Many helping interactions are quite transactional and end quickly. And that is okay. By being helpful, you are creating more opportunities than you had in the past to connect with new people, so the statistics still work in your favour.

In some situations it may not seem like anyone needs any help at all. But there will be other times when it is very clear how you could assist someone, and these occasions will jump out at you now that you've thought about being helpful.

STRATEGY FOUR: *How to Offer Help*

Notice What You Notice

If someone is struggling to get through a door with a handful of bags and perhaps a child in tow, you'll notice. If a jacket falls off the back of a chair while two people are deep into conversation, you'll notice. If someone slips on ice and flops to the ground such that you have to fight back laughter while feeling genuine concern, you'll notice that too. It's as if special forces have given you a sign or a sudden break from routine as a helpful reminder that you can more easily engage with that particular person. Or maybe it's just a coincidence. Who knows? And who cares? What is most important is how you respond to the need for help. The Meditator's Mindset will support you here because the more present you are, the more things you will notice.

Be Spontaneous and Act

Say "May I help you with that?" (Or modify this to be most appropriate for your situation.) If they say yes, then forget the dialogue in your head. Just jump into action and hold the door, pick up the scarf or the dropped change, or give up your seat on the train for someone who needs it more than you do. Do whatever the situation requires to be of service. In doing so, you create a space to connect. These acts of common courtesy stand out because they're no longer that common. They show that you care, that you are willing to be of service to other people, and that you are good person to talk to.

Do whatever the situation requires to be of service. In doing so, you create a space to connect.

Be Respectful and Get Consent

Not everyone who looks like they need help wants to be helped. Use your best judgment and learn by trial and error. Please always ask and respect whatever their answer is. If someone says no to your offer to help, leave them alone. If you help without consent, the person could be embarrassed or agitated. They likely won't be interested in speaking further. At other times, a kind gesture of help will seem like a divine act of fate that allowed you to meet a person.

Volunteer

If you are not comfortable with such a random method of helping, you could volunteer for a cause that you are already interested in. When you volunteer, you gain access to people you would not otherwise have an opportunity to meet, and you support your community as well. Studies indicate that people who volunteer experience mental and physical health benefits.[45]

It is important that your volunteering activities don't exceed your time and capacity to help. When this happens, you won't experience the many benefits of helping.

Small helpful gestures, as described above, can have a big impact. Seek them out and you will begin to notice them daily. Act on them when you can to become a helping hero as well as a connecting machine.

By helping a stranger, a conversation often naturally evolves. When you help someone boost their engine, push them out of a snowbank on the first snowfall of the year, or assist in any of the infinite ways possible, you are instantly engaged in that situation with them. You become a part of their experience and part of the solution. This will automatically have you in their good books because not everybody who noticed this situation stopped to offer any help. But you did!

We all need to slow down to stay connected to our humanity and help each other out. By doing so, you don't give up anything of yourself, yet you make an outstanding contribution. The satisfaction that comes from helping out is usually payment enough, but often new relationships can develop from these "chance" encounters. That's how I met Ryan Jeans.

One sunny May afternoon in 2012 while I was out on my balcony in Kensington, Toronto, I noticed a bearded man in his thirties was setting up sound equipment for an event. He hollered up to me, "Hey. Is there any power up there? Can I plug in?"

I replied, "Sure." Ryan was a member of a Brazilian band, Uma Nota, and they were about to play a concert in the yard right behind my apartment. Toronto's Kensington is colourful, cluttered, and cool. This is a good spot for such an event, I thought.

That unexpected interaction changed my life. We had a lot in common. We both knew construction, we both liked parties, and we were both playful people.

Helping Ryan took next to no effort on my part and I attended his concert. The following week, he kindly offered to help me at a book launch event that I was hosting. After meeting me only once, Ryan picked up and paid for the event's sound equipment—that I didn't even realize I needed. He also spent hours assisting me on the day. I was impressed by this kindness from a stranger. We became friends.

A few months later, there was a vacancy in his house and I moved in. While there, we started playing Ping-Pong on my kitchen table using a retractable net. Ryan loved this so much that he built a 3' x 6' tabletop for his studio. We played there too. Instantly hooked on the fun of miniature and portable Ping-Pong, he built more tables. Ryan brought these "miniPong" tables to various events and started getting hired to do so. He launched a business, miniPong.ca, and I moved out west to Alberta just in time for the epic floods of 2013.

We maintained our friendship. Whenever I visited family in London, Ontario, I was sure to visit Toronto as well.

By meeting Ryan, I got a place to live and a new friend who was also passionate about play. Ryan discovered his passion and has brought play to thousands of people. We have helped each other through many collaborations. Thanks to working with my father when I was young, I knew the basics of construction, so together we worked on Ryan's renovation, and he eventually opened a bed and breakfast. That is how he met his lovely Japanese wife Yayoi, and I've enjoyed witnessing them raise their son together as well.

Of course, not all of these events are a direct result of helping that day, but you can see how they are all connected. He used help to say hi to me, which started a ripple effect of positivity. Neither of us knew at the time that this chance meeting would lead to such a rich and important friendship, but we were both open to the possibility.

Ryan says, "Most neighbours and people in big cities look the other way when you ask for help because they think, *Ah, now I've got to say hello to this guy every day.* But there's something special about it being in a different setting with a stranger. It allows people to be people."

How might you offer help to start an interaction with someone? I challenge you to open a door, give up a seat, share your power, offer genuine courtesy, or simply say yes when someone asks you for help. Where might that interaction lead?

Asking for Help

Many of us are programmed to believe that asking for help is a sign of weakness and something that we should never do. In a 2015 survey of 2,214 men in Alberta, "Nearly 1 in 3 respondents would not seek support due to pressures of traditional masculinity."[46]

Another reason that people don't ask for help is that we don't think people will want to help us. We expect to get rejected. According to psychologist Heidi Grant, "We wildly underestimate how likely people are to help."[47] According to Alison Wood Brooks and Francesca Gino in their article "Asking Advice Makes a Good Impression," "Fears about appearing incompetent by asking for advice—though extremely common—are sorely misplaced. Here's why: when you ask for advice, people do not think less of you, they actually think you're *smarter*. By asking someone to share his or her personal wisdom, advice seekers stroke the advisor's ego and can gain valuable insights."[48] So ask for help. Here's a story about what good can come from asking for advice.

T2MP Day 287

I was with my friend Jude, whom I've known for almost forty years, at the Williams Coffee Pub in downtown London, Ontario. On that day, I was in no mood to meet a random stranger, so I did it anyway. To our left, I saw an elderly man sitting by himself and I decided to say hello.

This was my approach. "Excuse me. May I ask you a quick question?"

"Yes," he replied. "I'm just about to turn forty-two years old and I still haven't figured life out. You seem to be a few years older than me, so I was wondering: Could you tell me what you think I should do?"

He kind of laughed a little and replied in a thick Irish accent with a bunch of questions:

"Have you got a job?" "Yes."

"Do you volunteer?" "Yes."

"Maybe you need to travel?" "I have travelled."

"Perhaps you should join a theatre group." "I am in one now."

This entertaining rapid-fire Q & A had me laughing, as it made me feel I had pretty great things going on in my life already.

And then Sean slapped me with words that surprised me. "Well, maybe you just need to settle down."

This was so interesting for me to hear. Parents and friends had told me this before, but coming from an old, wise man with an accent—a total stranger —the suggestion seemed to have more weight.

I liked how he said, "You know, it's a good idea to look towards the next ten years. And when you hit fifty-two, if you can say, 'That was a good decade,' then you'll be doing pretty well."

Jude had overheard the conversation, so we talked about it back at our table. He told me that he also benefited from the wisdom just from listening to us chat.

On his way out, Sean very respectfully came to our table. He shook my hand, looked me in the eyes and said, "Good luck to ya." I was deeply affected by his kindness. I could feel that this man actually cared for me, even though I was a stranger. "Thank you so much for the conversation, Sean. It was great to meet you."

Answering a random request for advice was no inconvenience to him, and it led to such a gift for each of us. Now, that's an information gift exchange!

If you have grown up with the limiting beliefs that it's unmanly, bothersome, or weak to ask for help or advice, how can you get past them?

STRATEGY FIVE: *How to Ask for Help*
Ask a Person, Not Your "Smart" Device

Sure, we can find the answer to almost any question by accessing the internet in the palm of our hand (or with a voice command), but that doesn't mean it's the best way to get answers. At this stage, think about how else you might ask for help. What you are looking for are small excuses to have more human interaction, so don't overthink it.

Is there something that you could use assistance with?

Do you need directions to a hiking/scrambling route or a hostel or hotel recommendation? How about asking where the nearest organic market is? You can even ask the time when you intentionally leave your devices at home.

Be Specific

Be specific about what you ask. This makes it easy for the recipient of your request to understand what you need and to respond accordingly.

A vague request: "Can you help me with something?"

A specific request: "Can you guide me to the nearest public washroom?"

Use the Word "Quick" in Your Request

Say something along the lines of "May I ask you for a quick piece of advice about X?" By including the word "quick," you indicate that you won't take much of their time. You're being respectful and also making it easier for the person to say yes to your request, in the scenario that they're not able or willing to commit much time to doing you a favour.

Don't Apologize for Asking for Help

In her article "A Social Psychologist Explains Why We Should Ask for Help More Often," Angela Chen quotes Heidi Grant: "Another thing that backfires is profusely apologizing for asking. You're so focused on your own feeling of apologizing, and then I'm starting to feel icky, and it robs me of my ability to enjoy helping because you're so busy putting yourself down about needing help."[49] Just ask for help when you need it. Keep your apologies handy for when you properly screw something up.

Be Ready for Whatever Response Comes Up

Become okay with rejection, as it will happen sometimes. Don't think of that as a failure. Rather, it's a victory that you worked up the courage to ask for help. It's part of learning a new skill. Give yourself a high-five no matter what.

Thank Them and Follow Up

If you exchange contact information with the person you meet, be sure to follow up and let them know what actions you took if they gave you help or advice. This can create another opportunity to connect and to offer and receive further help as well. More specifics on how to follow up are in the next chapter, "Keep (the Conversation) Going."

If after reading all of this, you still don't think that asking for help is a good idea, what will happen if you are hurt or in danger? Will you swallow your pride and ask then? Here's a story about when I had to ask for help.

T2MP Day 302

Today I met four people in the Temple Lodge while snowboarding at Lake Louise. I asked, "Can you let me know if you think I have a concussion?"

"What are your symptoms?" a man replied. "Are you dizzy, tired, or spaced out? How much do you remember? Did you black out?"

I had all of those symptoms.

Two of these people shared stories about being concussed. Then one of them stated, "If there's any question at all, you should go to first aid and get checked out." That was a good call.

So I did. In a medical building/tent, Alex treated me and she asked a few questions. I was out of it. She checked out my head and concluded that I had suffered a concussion.

I'm sure that you won't need to have an accident in order to meet people. But in my case, asking for help led to an interaction with strangers, and I got the information that I needed at the time for my own well-being. If I wasn't concussed, I'm sure we could have enjoyed a really good chat. When you need help, ask for it.

At the beginning of 2017, this accident stopped me from working for several weeks and it took me years to fully recover. That was extremely challenging, as I enjoyed and was used to a fast-paced life. I would eventually understand how that smack on the helmet was a blessing in disguise. I learned the hard lesson that if you don't slow down when you need to, life will force you.

Now I do less, have time for myself every day, and accomplish more. It has also influenced how I interact with people today. When I was younger, I had a much more selfish approach to interacting with people. I didn't fully buy in to the concept of "givers gain" and could lose interest if it seemed that there wasn't something of value for me in a discussion. But now I do the opposite. I am constantly seeking opportunities to help people out or connect them with someone in my network. It is now much easier to establish meaningful relationships with new people because I'm genuinely interested in being of service to them. This would not have become the case if I never slowed down. A new pace of life was forced upon me, which was exactly what I needed. Slowing down was one of the greatest impacts the Talk2MorePeople Project had on me. Slowing down also helped me learn how to ask for help.

Talk2MorePeople Listening

Though it may be more intimidating to approach multiple people, it might be easier in some cases to join an ongoing conversation than to initiate a conversation and guess what subject is most likely to interest a stranger standing on their own. This is because an established topic gives you the necessary clues to join in while Talk2MorePeople Listening. Yes, it takes more courage to approach more than one person, but you might actually prefer it.

STRATEGY SIX: *How to Use Talk2MorePeople Listening*

Until now, when hearing such conversations, you have most likely kept your juicy mind-thoughts to yourself. But in every moment of every day, you have the opportunity to create new behaviour. And now it's time for you to be heard, so use your voice. It's time for you to make a contribution to this conversation and to get over the fear of doing so.

When you act spontaneously, you act authentically, and how polished your approach is matters less than how genuine you are.

When you notice a familiar discussion point/subject—one that you can relate to because you've studied it; cried tears over it; been there, done that, got the T-shirt; hiked the mountain; effectively lived the experience being discussed—it is your golden moment to join the conversation. But this moment won't last long, because it's easy to talk yourself out of it. I strongly encourage you to embrace your inner child and follow the impulse to chime in right away when something you hear resonates with you. Once again, when you act spontaneously, you act authentically, and how polished your approach is matters less than how genuine you are.

So take a breath, put on a smile, make eye contact, and gently break into the conversation. You can wait for an appropriate break in the discussion, but you don't need to. Say to the people you overheard talking, "Excuse me. I just overheard you speaking about X." And then follow up with, "May I add...," "I'd like to add...," or "I'd like to comment on..." Go ahead. Jump in. You can do it. Remember that research has proven that they are more likely to approve of you than you expect.

Other useful phrases to have in your back pocket include: "Can you tell me more about...," "I have a quick question about...," "Do you know if...," and "Have you heard about..."

You don't have to say exactly these words when you meet a new person, but I've used phrases like this dozens of times and they do work. You need to truly believe that you have a contribution to make, and you will soon see that you do.

If the people you approached don't seem interested in speaking with you or don't respond, don't panic! You can excuse yourself, move along, and find other people to meet. If they welcome you with open body language and engage in dialogue with you, enjoy! You've just joined a conversation and met new people. How to keep that conversation going is coming up next in the "Keep (the Conversation) Going" chapter.

A Talk2MorePeople Listening Example

Here's an example of how you can turn thoughts into words spoken aloud:

What you're thinking: *What a delicious coffee. I wonder what those people are talking about? I can hear them a little. Oh. The Calgary folk music festival? I've been there before! I can relate to that. I even applied to volunteer once, but a gig got in the way. I'd love to join their conversation, but how do I do it? Can I just walk up and start talking with them about Folk Fest?*

What you can say: "Excuse me. I just overheard you talking about the Calgary folk music festival. I once signed up to volunteer for it. I love Folk Fest." Now you're in, and you've got their attention. But if they don't respond right away, how can you invite the back-and-forth that will keep this new conversation alive?

Use questions. You can circle back to the beginning of this chapter and apply those tips to a group setting as well.

In the Folk Fest example above, you could ask, "Are you going this year?"

Strangers: "Yes, we will be there. We haven't missed it for ten years..."

And this leads you to a really enjoyable conversation. Congratulations. Enjoy the music.

Listen

 Overcome
Internal Obstacles

 Open a Dialogue
—Six Strategies

 Keep (the Conversation)
Going

 Uncomfortable?
How to Exit a Conversation

 Play and Improvise

Keep (the Conversation) Going

K: KEEP (THE CONVERSATION) GOING

Success is stumbling from failure to failure
with no loss of enthusiasm.
—*Winston S. Churchill*

At times you may think, *Well, I interrupted them with my question or comment,*
and we have started a conversation. But what do we talk about now? What is this
person's worldview? What matters to them? How do I get past this stressful monologue
in my head? Are they happy to speak with me or a little annoyed? This is bizarre!

From students, I hear some version of this all the time: "I am able to meet
people, but what next?" First of all, congratulations! The difficult part is
over—you got the conversation started.

Secondly, yes, it is a little bizarre. Nobody can tell you precisely what to
say once you are suddenly in an unexpected conversation because every
single encounter will be different. People are so wonderfully varied in
culture, disposition, attitude, and life experience that you will have to play
with each situation and see where it leads. It is fine to bring in ideas or even
a starting phrase or two, but if you bring a script, you may come across as
inauthentic. And nobody wants that.

You can get past the stressful monologue in your head by turning your
attention to any of the techniques that you learned about in the "Open a
Dialogue" chapter. Pick something that is not too much of a stretch for you
and see where it takes you.

But if you are still feeling anxious, just become aware that you are feeling
that way and verbally acknowledge it. This awareness and other resources
can help reduce the anxiety. Eventually you will be able to separate yourself
from the anxious thoughts and regain control. Visit AnxietyCanada.com
for free resources to support you if you struggle with anxiety.

For sure it would be nice if every interaction was blissful, but not every
conversation needs to be or can be a great one. There will be flops and
times when you or the other person wants to escape. That's fine. It's
normal. Don't let it stress you out.

This chapter is here to support you, to help you benefit from the efforts
you have already put into any project that you have been working on. Too
often, time and energy are wasted on something that seemed like a good
idea to start out with but never saw its way through to completion. So let's
keep the conversation going.

How to Extend a Conversation
and Make it More Impactful

Just Be You

Allow yourself to be as present, curious, adventurous, adaptable, and spontaneous as feels natural to you. See what happens. Let the mystery of life show you the way. Once a conversation has started, trust that you will hear topics that are of interest to you. Build on this new information. While communicating with someone, at times it's like the movie *Inception,* where an idea is placed in a person's mind in order to create a new outcome.

Stay Focused on the Person

Show that you are interested in what the person is speaking about. Don't look over their shoulder to see what is going on around them. Maintain eye contact when you are speaking with them (unless this goes against the cultural norm). Put that device down in the other room or chuck it out the window and give them the gift of your full attention. You will stand out as caring and genuine by doing so.

Put that device down in the other room or chuck it out the window and give them the gift of your full attention.

Let Them Share

The skills that you picked up from the earlier tools will support you here. When you don't know what to say in a conversation, you can ask questions to keep the conversation moving forward. Many people love talking about themselves. And asking questions helps build rapport and takes the pressure off of you to figure out what to say. Just don't ask so many questions that it seems like an interrogation. Be sure to share as well.

As they talk, listen for references to places, passions, activities, or past events. If you can identify what is important to the other person, then you will be able to extend the conversation by asking follow-up questions. If you notice their face looks happier or "lights up" when they mention something, that is a bright, shiny clue to explore further. You can also follow your curiosity. What words pique your interest? When these words catch your attention, it is your opportunity to ask them to share a little more. And if you don't get a chance to ask a question when it comes to mind, make a mental or actual note and ask it later. It is very positive to ask a person to expand upon something that they said earlier. They will likely appreciate that you thought something they said was important enough for you to remember.

Ask Deep Questions

Try asking why they are here—as in on the planet—if you really want to get into it. You never know how willing they will be to get into a real conversation. A "real" conversation has depth to it and will leave one or both parties reflecting or commenting on it to others once it's concluded. (That is not to say that an "unreal" conversation is not worthwhile—only that it will likely have a lesser impact on the participants.)

Let me tell you about Jan Keck. A German man who'd recently settled in Toronto, he was having little luck creating meaningful relationships out of encounters at the events he was attending. After time passed, he decided to start asking people deeper questions even if it at times it seemed inappropriate. The response he got was telling. Not everyone he asked a deep question was interested in such a discussion, but many people were. In fact, some people said that they were relieved to not have to bother with small talk. This also led to many new and meaningful relationships.

He then created the Ask Deep Questions card deck, which, at the time of writing, has sold 1,776 decks worldwide. I have a set of his cards, and they are great. The questions range from curious to brave to vulnerable. Here is how Jan recommends using the cards: "You need to build trust over time before two strangers will feel safe to be vulnerable with each other. That's why I always recommend starting with curious, then brave, and then vulnerable." After using the cards several times, people notice that they engage in much less small talk and enjoy more deep, meaningful conversations with both friends and strangers. Take a look at the wonderful work Jan Keck is doing and, if you like, grab a set of his cards at AskDeepQuestions.com.

It doesn't have to take weeks or months to get to know somebody well. Yes, certain encounters can develop smoothly from small talk. But you can also ask deep questions. Dare to discover what's really important to the person you are speaking with. Finding the right timing to ask such questions comes with practice.

Be Vulnerable

While it is important to listen and let the other person share, dare to be vulnerable by sharing something about yourself too. You don't want to seem as if you are conducting an interview or leading an interrogation by asking too many questions. See if you can create somewhat of an equal balance in the conversation between listening and sharing.

How to Build Long-Term Relationships
from Brief Encounters

1. Ask for Contact Information

If you have just had an enjoyable random interaction with someone new in public or at a networking event (in person or online), and you would like to remain connected, ask for their contact information even if you've already given them yours. People are so lovely, bless their hearts. But don't expect that they'll contact you even if the encounter was positive. People get busy, forget, feel awkward if they didn't contact you when they say they were going to, avoid it, and occasionally simply don't care enough to keep in touch. All of this is possible even if you had a swimmingly good chat.

So take the initiative yourself. It is your responsibility to do so. The worst that they can say is no. And if that happens, they just saved you time by telling you honestly that they don't want to remain in contact. How many times have you met someone interesting and as they walked away thought, *Darn. I'd really like to follow up with that person, but I didn't get their number?* Today more than ever, it is frightfully easy to find people online, but you will have a much better chance of a warm reply if the person actually gave you their contact information directly.

2. Follow Up

When someone has shared their contact information with you, there is a high likelihood that they too enjoyed your interaction and will be happy to hear from you. This is often the case even if you don't hear from them, so make sure they hear from you again.

Don't task a new contact with reading your life story when you follow up. Instead, be like a good idea: concise.

Following up strategically helps keep you connected. You can master all the skills in the world for how to meet people, but if you can't remain in contact with the people you connect with, you will be missing out on the main benefit—longer-term relationships.

Follow up by email—or better yet, by phone, if they prefer—within twenty-four hours of meeting them. Keep the promises you make to others and to yourself. If it requires scheduling for you to do this, schedule it.

In your follow-up message, do the following:

- Be specific: Mention something specific about your interaction so that it is easy for them to remember you. "I was the person wearing a mirror hat" seems to work well, for example. Including specific details in the first correspondence will also make it easier for you to remember your first interaction with that person in the future. It's like a note to yourself.

- Add value: Consider if there is any way that you can be of service to that other person. There are some great recommendations in the article "How to Follow Up After Meeting Someone in Person" on The Art of Manliness website.[50]

- Be concise: Cut to the chase. More senior employees and employers seem to write shorter emails and responses. Don't task a new contact with reading your life story when you follow up. Instead, be like a good idea: concise.

3. Follow Up Again

What happens if you don't hear back from a contact? It is easy to have doubts—don't be offended and don't worry about it. Just follow up again a few days or a week later. Once again, people are busy. If you can't reach them with your second follow-up, let it go. You may still hear from them in the future.

If you never hear back, that's okay too. Many more new connections are waiting for you even if it felt awkward or didn't work this time. Soon it will work! And you will begin to experience the magic that is possible when you Talk2MorePeople.

4. Make Use of What You Have Already Learned

Connecting with new people is a worthy endeavour on its own, but the many new ideas, experiences, and opportunities that you will discover are worth exploring further. Once you have shared or learned something in an information gift exchange, it's time to do something with that, so take action.

If you are given information that is relevant to your sphere of influence, then be sure to flag it, look it up, make the call, or visit the place. Take the first action that's possible to make use of the gift that you just received in your information exchange.

And when you take action based on what the person suggested, be sure to follow up with them again and let them know what you did. This step often gets missed when people are benefiting from other people's wisdom. It's important to do, however, because it shows the person who taught you something that you cared enough to take action with the information or advice they shared. This can lead to more opportunities to connect where everyone benefits.

5. Reconnect with Old Connections

A great suggestion that I received from Jesse Keefer on Galiano Island, BC, was how to maintain existing connections: "As soon as someone who you know pops into your mind, call them!" He does this often and it's helped him maintain a large social network.

Experiencing a Setback? What Now?

Continue to pursue this goal of learning to connect with strangers and you will likely have fun along the way. That is due to the quantity of untapped, unpredictable experiences that you will create by meeting people. It is very easy to become discouraged when learning a new skill; however, continuing to work at it can lead to success and, ultimately, mastery. That's why you must keep going. Until you start to do it, you may have no idea just how good meeting new people can be for you.

On my journey, there were times of self-doubt, depression, anxiety, and even despair. February 23, 2016, would have been my dear old dad's eightieth birthday. Several months earlier, during one particularly low point, with tears streaming down my face, I held on to his ashes and asked out loud, "Dad, what should I do?" Almost instantly I heard the answer: "Just keep going!"

It was as if my late father was really speaking to me. Or maybe it was my unconscious mind or another form of divine insight. Whatever it was, I got the message, and I kept going. I like to think that the message came from Dad. After all, it is something that he said in life too. Two months later, I began the Talk2MorePeople Project, which became the most important work that I had ever done.

"Keep (the Conversation) Going" is a strategy not only for making the most of Talk2MorePeople encounters but also for supporting you in overcoming personal or professional challenges through persistence. You will learn that when you know you've got important work to do, you do it. You keep at it. You treat your work as your top priority.

How to Keep Going After a Setback

Below are tips to help you progress further on your journey of human connection if you have hit roadblocks or not yet achieved the results you would like.

Is It Important to You?

Consider if what you are learning or doing is important to you. If meeting strangers is a task that you feel you *should* learn to do, but your heart truly isn't in it, it will be more difficult to develop this skill. Once you intentionally have your first encounter and experience the empowerment that comes with that, it will be easier to keep going.

Try a Different Approach

If you are using one or two of the strategies from this book that you are most comfortable with but aren't connecting with people, try something new. What else could you do to meet someone new? You could even say, "I am challenging myself to meet more people for my own good, so I thought that I'd approach you." This topic can become a subject of conversation on its own.

Try a Different Setting

It might be that your normal life patterns are fairly structured and predictable. You may need to shake things up by going to a different part of your city or town. Take another route to school or work, and allow unexpected encounters to occur. When you change the setting, it can help to change your mindset if you were feeling discouraged. You gift yourself a fresh start. Also, different places will attract different types of people.

Choose Your Timing Wisely

Some people say that timing is everything in life and, to a certain extent, I agree. It will usually be more challenging to make a connection with someone who is quickly moving down the street or obviously engaged in their own experience. The following encounter was a reminder to me that it really helps to approach people at the right time.

T2MP Day 321

Today at the new Red's Diner in Kensington, my housemate Josh Buyze noticed the Canadian Alpine Ski Team jackets worn by four people in the restaurant. He said that he had seen them at the Banff Hot Springs yesterday. I love mountains and winter sports—that's something I can relate to—and thought this would be a great opportunity to say hello, so I did. Unfortunately, my timing was off.

I approached their table and said, "Excuse me, may I ask you a quick question?" At the same moment, I realized their fourth plate of food was just being set down. They said yes but looked a little puzzled and possibly annoyed. "Were you at the Banff Hot Springs yesterday?" I asked. They shook their heads. I explained that my housemate thought that he had seen them there. Although I sensed that this was no time for a random conversation, I still asked two more quick questions: "Is being an alpine racer exciting? Do you love it?" This time, all four of them lit up with smiles. One of them said, "Yeah, it's pretty awesome!"

"Oh, that's what I thought. Thank you very much. Enjoy your lunch." And then I left the situation.

This encounter showed me that conversations can still happen under not-so-ideal circumstances, though they might feel a little awkward if you time your approach poorly, as I did. But that's okay. Tomorrow is another day, and there will be a new conversation.

Take a Break and Try, Try Again

During the Talk2MorePeople Project, I had to meet at least one new person a day, every day, for a full year. Did I get rejected? Yes. Did that stop me? No. The only way I could meet people daily was to try, try again. If I approached a person or group of people who I couldn't get into a conversation with, I had to make another attempt at it. But not with the same people, and not right away. Before rushing into another encounter, I'd take a longer version of the "one-second break" to regroup. I had to learn a lesson from the Meditator's Mindset.

Practise

Go to events where there are people and do your best. The more attempts you make at it, the more comfortable you will begin to feel. Remember that you are learning a new skill, so it won't necessarily be easy starting off. But keep at it, and it can eventually become as easy as breathing.

Setbacks generally don't feel good. So how do you keep going if you experience rejection when trying your best to meet new people? Remember that it's okay to drop the ball. Watch any skilled juggler perform. They will dazzle you as they manipulate objects in the air in patterns that you can hardly understand as you watch. It can be easy to lose sight of the fact that every juggler has dropped thousands of balls on their journey to mastery. As you know, making mistakes is a necessary part of the learning process. There is no need to fear it or allow it to make you uncomfortable any longer.

T2MP Day 79

People sometimes ask, "Did you ever miss a day?" I did. Once. Did that stop me? No. Having recently tapered off my antidepressants, my mind and body were unpredictable. I couldn't count on having my typical positive attitude on any given day. The antidepressants were a last resort after an incident that took place after three years of talk therapy. For weeks, my attitude was hit-or-miss.

On Day 79 of the Talk2MorePeople Project, I dropped the ball. After meeting a new stranger every single day for two and a half months, while dealing with financial instability, a concussion, and withdrawal from the meds, I was mentally and physically exhausted. On that day, I didn't leave the house.

Missing one day of a challenge can be extremely discouraging because you've already put so much effort in. Then you slip up and it's like, "Shoot. It's over! I failed."

But one miss doesn't have to equal total failure. In a perfect world, we would all complete our projects as planned, on budget and on time. But we don't live in a perfect world. Today more than ever, we live in a world of rapid change, so that's not always possible. Situations change with little notice and so do the results. So, at times, you need to cut yourself a little slack.

On that day, I made a short video about my experience.[51] It was the first time I stated publicly that I had been dealing with depression, and that terrified me. The next day, I got back to meeting people.

I redid Day 79 and continued the challenge with more determination than ever. I was proud of the project even though for one day it was too much for me. Knowing the importance of consistency in challenges, I was careful not to let this one fall keep me down. I didn't miss another day of meeting a person for the full year. ☺

To get back up from this one crash, I modified my behaviour to accomplish my goals. I considered what was working and what was not. I started to meet people earlier in the day and made a conscious decision not to consider myself a failure. That fall became my fuel.

When it got late in the day and I had not yet met anyone, I would stop what I was doing and get outside. This happened after midnight at times and still led to great new connections.

Missing one day of a challenge should not stop you from enjoying the benefits down the line. Yes, consistency matters, but perfection is unrealistic. Anticipating that failure is just part of the process should make it easier for you to continue. So keep going.

> # Missing one day of a challenge should not stop you from enjoying the benefits down the line. Yes, consistency matters, but perfection is unrealistic.

How to Keep Going When You Think You Can't Start

Just Start

If you feel stuck in the Talk2MorePeople listening stage—where you overhear discussions that you could join—or if you feel like you are too in your head for this, take a moment and break the task down. At this stage, what is going on anyhow? You are trying to meet new people. Identify what the first, smallest (and therefore totally possible) step for you is, and then commit yourself to doing only that small step. This can keep that sense of overwhelm at a distance. It's like playing a mind trick on yourself: *Hey. You only need take what you've overheard and write it down*—do that *Talk2MorePeople Listening*—*or share it with a supportive friend to get closer to actually meeting someone. You don't have to say anything to a stranger yet. Sometimes getting started is more difficult than the task you are avoiding.*

Often, when the first small step is complete, it's much easier to decide upon the next small step and eventually build momentum to complete the task.

Persist, Even If You Don't Feel Like It

Getting great results in life takes effort. That doesn't mean that it must feel like hard work all the time, but unless you inherited a fortune, discipline will likely be required.

In *The War of Art,* Steven Pressfield suggests that you show up and do your work every day whether you feel up to it or not. No excuses. Pressfield differentiates between the amateur and the professional. The amateur talks about the work that they are doing, and the professional is the one who shows up to do their important work even when they don't feel like it. At this stage of your journey, are you an amateur or a pro? His book is inspiring and very helpful for anyone who has ever been stuck on a project. In fact, it helped me complete this book.

Persistence in what you choose to do will help you do more than you think is possible and it will be good for you. When you keep at something, the energy behind your efforts leads to better results, even if, at times, it feels like you are going nowhere. Most overnight success stories happen for people who have been working at their craft for years. Another great resource on this subject is *The Compound Effect* by Darren Hardy, which shows how making small, incremental changes, and being consistent with them, can create transformation in just about any area of your life.

Learning to Meet People Is Just Like Riding a Bicycle

Here is a short story of persistence:

Did you learn to ride a bicycle as a child? Did you fall? Of course you did. Did that stop you from learning? Not likely. You learned to ride a bicycle with persistence *despite* falling.

I'd like to time-travel back to my 2008 cross-Canada bike tour mentioned earlier. I was travelling with Julian. Because of his German accent (which sounds similar to Schwarzenegger's Austrian accent) and his admirable strength (he often carried my luggage on his bike), he earned the name "The Terminator." This was especially amusing when he needed an eye patch for an injury that he got on the trip.

We made it to Vancouver on schedule, but I suffered an injury on the third day. I had to hitchhike about 350 km with my bike and trailer just to catch up with him. After a rest, I decided to continue despite the injury because the tour was important to me.

It was both a physical and psychological challenge. We sometimes had to wake up at 5 a.m. to avoid the assault of westerly winds. This was discouraging to say the least. At times, pushing with all of our strength, we could only go 10 km/hour. This brought me to tears. I complained about my exhausted legs. Julian—a professionally trained athlete—would tell me: "Screw your legs! You don't have a weakness of the body. You have a weakness of the mind!"

He was right, and this message helped me to keep going. Even when there are setbacks, you can accomplish a challenging task if you persist at it even when it seems impossible. I had what I needed to physically do the trip, but I needed a push to fix my mindset. Cycling this distance was possible. After all, other people had done it. And eventually so did we. The same applies when you set out to meet new people.

—

Now you have more tips to keep you—and your conversation—going. Be mindful that becoming an expert conversationalist is not something that one can achieve overnight.

In life, it can be easy to be hard on ourselves, and hard to be easy on ourselves. When you make efforts to connect with someone—even if it didn't lead to a conversation or a new connection—celebrate that! If it's new behaviour for you, this is huge. Don't sell yourself short of a celebration that you deserve. Celebrate the rewards that will eventually come from your courageous efforts. Keep going.

Listen

 Overcome
Internal Obstacles

 Open a Dialogue
—Six Strategies

 Keep (the Conversation)
Going

 Uncomfortable?
How to Exit a Conversation

 Play and Improvise

Uncomfortable?

How to Exit a Conversation

U: UNCOMFORTABLE? HOW TO EXIT A CONVERSATION _____

The most compassionate people have the strongest boundaries.
—Brené Brown

T2MP Day 209

My final encounter with a stranger today was unlike any other so far on this journey. I arrived home by bicycle at 10:45 p.m. and found someone walking up the alley and into my backyard. Instantly my heart started racing. The man, who was about my size, quickly came out of the darkness and gestured to shake my hand. I told him that wasn't necessary. My guard was up. My eyes sharply focused on him as he darted around the yard. I could see that he was a little rough around the edges.

He asked, "Is this your house?"

"Yes," I replied in a firmer-than-normal tone. "What do you need?"

"I stored my bag in your yard and I'm trying to find it," he said.

"What do you mean?" I asked.

"I got hustled and into a fight earlier tonight after I left the drop-in centre." He seemed confused and scattered.

"Are you okay?" I asked. "Yes," he answered. We used a bicycle light to look through my yard and my neighbours' yard for the bag that may or may not have existed.

All this time I wondered if he was on drugs or planning to jump me. He had cuts on his face and dirty hands. I was conflicted because I really wanted to help him but felt that he could be a threat. We spent about five minutes together and found no bag.

"Here, take this bike light. You should stay out of people's yards at night," I told him.

"Thanks, man, I know."

Then we did shake hands and I asked, "What's your name?"

"It's Eric. I'll return the light later," he said, and then he was on his way. As I watched him head down the alley, my heart rate started returning to normal.

Once I got inside the house, I thought, I should have offered him food. But that didn't occur to me because I was concerned about my own safety. I haven't experienced that heightened state of "fight or flight" for years. I know, based upon how my body felt in those minutes with him, that I was ready for a physical encounter if one suddenly started. My adrenaline was pumping.

Of course, there's a good chance his story was completely legitimate and there was no threat. It's very difficult to say.

Was I right to feel threatened by a rough guy who was in my yard late in the evening? Probably. But how often does a person like this—who might have no bad intentions, just a streak of very bad luck or mental health or addiction challenges—get unnecessarily categorized as a threat? It is something to think about when we see people who look different than us. Even if you never read this, I wish you all the best, Eric. Please take care of yourself.

I felt uncomfortable during my conversation with this stranger because I felt that my safety was at risk. Despite that, I engaged with him and everything was fine. If you go on a meeting-people marathon, there will likely be times when you land in uncomfortable conversations. But an uncomfortable conversation isn't always threatening, as we saw above. So, for a few moments, let's dive into this discomfort.

Conversations Can Get Uncomfortable

Situations may arise when you feel uncomfortable in a conversation with someone new or someone you already know, and it's helpful to have strategies to get out of those situations. Later in this chapter, I'll also show you how to read the signs that you aren't welcome in a discussion and help you exit those conversations too.

But before we get to the words you can say and the actions you can take, let's examine why you may stay in an uncomfortable conversation and work on improving that mindset first.

Do you have a compulsion to make sure that everyone is happy? It was one of mine for years. It's a great quality to have unless it holds you back from taking care of your own needs. People pleasers often feel held hostage in conversations that they don't want to be in, and they stay because they don't want to upset anyone or be perceived as rude. Of course, it is ideal to be polite, and nobody wants to burn bridges, but many people worry more than is necessary. And, in any event, you shouldn't discount your own happiness. If you experience these conflicted thoughts, allow yourself to notice when this happens. That awareness, along with other tips listed here, can help you to become comfortable leaving when you want to.

When hosting events, I remind the participants that they are under no obligation to stay in a conversation that they don't want to be in for any reason. I set up a safe space for people to leave the situation and move on to speak with someone else. This reminds participants that they always have permission to exit a conversation. The trick is to get comfortable leaving even when nobody gives permission. Exiting a conversation without permission can be done in public, but if you've never done it before, it will take practice.

Being compassionate means that you communicate what you need and you don't give more than you can of yourself.

Another reason you might hesitate to leave a conversation is that you're not used to saying no. People with a sense of adventure and lots of curiosity may have a desire to experience everything. As a person who used to attend three or four events in the same night, I am all too familiar with this feeling. A self-proclaimed "yes man," I had to learn how to say no for my own good and to stop being a people pleaser. This took and still takes practice.

When you are asked to do someone a favour, really think about if you can actually manage it before you say yes. It all comes back to taking care of yourself. You can't truly be of service to anyone else unless you have your own energy under control. Serve yourself and then serve others. Being compassionate means that you communicate what you need and you don't give more than you can of yourself.

How to Exit an Uncomfortable Conversation

While you are conversation hunting, you never know what you are going to catch. This creates both fun and fear. Unfortunately, some conversations can become uncomfortable.

Here are some methods that you can use to exit a conversation. Every situation is unique, so different tips will be useful in different situations. Remember to experiment, take care of your own needs, and use your best judgment.

Use Closed Body Language

An easy way to start—which doesn't require any words at all—is to use closed body language.

- Make less eye contact. Good eye contact is one way that we can build rapport and show that we are intently listening to what the other person is saying. Avoiding eye contact has the opposite effect.

- Change the position of your body so that you are no longer directly facing the other person. When you position yourself as if you need to get away, they will often pick up on this. This includes pointing your feet away from the other person.

- Nodding is one way that we show engagement while conversing, so nod less and they might get the hint that you are not into the discussion. A glossed-over gaze will do the same trick.

- Cross your arms instead of resting them on the chair, the table, or your lap. Sit back if you are in a chair or step back if you are standing to physically move farther away from the other person.

- Start looking down at your phone. It's a handy conversation stopper.

Frame Your Exit as a Favour

Say, "Well, I won't keep you any longer" or "So, I'd better let you go" or "I won't take any more of your time." These statements indicate that you value the other person's time and you need to leave so as to not occupy any more of it (even though, in fact, you are doing this for yourself and for your freedom from the encounter).

Don't Justify Your Exit

You can also just politely say, "Excuse me," and leave the situation. Resist the temptation to justify or provide an excuse for your departure. Often when people explain why they can't keep a commitment, or why they need out of something, there is a lie involved. Why would you let someone else make you lie? Don't give them that power. Just excuse yourself and move on. They will get over it.

Even if you do have a second reason to leave the situation (in addition to no longer wanting to engage in conversation)—maybe you need to suddenly floss, go to the washroom, or get food—you could express that as a legitimate excuse to leave if it makes you feel better, but there's no need to. Let go of your sense of obligation to this person.

Pass It On

Introduce the person to someone new. If you are at a function or a networking event, you can ask someone nearby if they have had a chance to meet the person you are speaking with. It would be best if they have something in common, but this doesn't have to be the case. Once they start conversing, you can excuse yourself and slip away.

Perhaps the problem with getting stuck in unwanted conversations has less to do with not knowing how to exit than it does with being unable or unwilling to use your voice.

Interrupt the Monologue

You can interrupt the speaker and change the subject. I'm giving you permission to do so. In a group setting, if you are bored or uncomfortable with the discussion, it is likely that someone else is as well. You have the choice to continue to suffer through the dumping of pointless, irrelevant, or worse material, or to take action. You can take control by interrupting with a confident voice. It's best to wait for a pause, but that's not always possible.

Time and human connection are two of our most valuable resources. Don't give them away out of complacency.

Some people never stop talking, so say this, "Sorry to interrupt you, I wanted to share..." or "Sorry to interrupt you, I'd like to comment that..." If you facilitate events, you are likely familiar with the use of "[Rambling person's name], I'm just going to pause you for a moment..." and this stops the monologue. You can use this technique in online meetings as well.

You can also question a nearby person about something else to stop the Chatty Cathy and shift the focus to another speaker. Even if this has been a sensitive issue for you in the past, don't be afraid to use your voice. Wasting your precious time accommodating others can cost you your own growth.

On the other hand, if you would rather end the conversation than change the topic, say, "I'm sorry to interrupt you, but I'm off now" or "Thank you for your thoughts. I've got to get going now," and then exit the situation. Time and human connection are two of our most valuable resources. Don't give them away out of complacency.

Speak Up If You Are Offended

There are many reasons why people don't speak up when they are offended, including shock, concern about personal safety, and avoidance of conflict. In the article "How to Speak Up When It Matters," authors Khalil Smith, Heidi Grant, and David Rock suggest saying something like this, "You may not have meant to offend, but here is how I experienced that joke."[52] That is a clear and non-confrontational way to let someone know that you felt uncomfortable with what was said. By doing so, you help educate the offender on what's acceptable to say and what's not. But don't worry so much about speaking up properly. If you are offended, you deserve to express it.

Use Your Voice

It is empowering to be authentic, so speak whatever is on your mind. For many reasons we often don't use our voice even when we really want to. It's as if there is something stuck in our throat that stops us from speaking our mind. This can be self-limiting in many areas of life because leaving situations without expressing yourself can cause regret and frustration.

What you have to say and offer is of value, even if you don't feel that way. As you will experience when you have an information gift exchange with someone new, you make a positive contribution. Sometimes it will feel easy and other times—around other people—it may seem impossible.

Growing up a shy child, I used to always keep my thoughts to myself. It's not that I thought what I had to say was unimportant; rather, I wasn't sure that it was okay to speak up. I always felt I needed permission from someone else to make a contribution. But I managed to outgrow the tendency by actually using my voice more and more, starting in my late teens. At first I spoke up more often with the people I already knew. Gradually, my reach expanded further, and since then, life has continued to improve.

You can go a step further and take a page from my father's book. Be completely honest with people, all of the time. Do you know how much weight you carry by putting on a facade with acquaintances you would really rather not spend time with? Tell it like it is, like my father did. But don't be rude about it. Although not everybody liked this quality of his, they respected him and his honesty. This level of honesty saves you time and energy in life. Aim for your comments to land in that sweet spot between softly using your voice and surprising the person with how boldly you speak up. (They don't need to know that you might be even more surprised.)

Of course, this might not make you the most popular person, so gauge how outspoken you want to be. Keep in mind that you don't need to *raise* your voice to *use* your voice. But by expressing your true self, more aligned souls will begin to show up in your life.

How to Read the Signs of Another Person's Discomfort

The tips I've just shared will help you control how much time you spend in social situations. There is no need for you to feel trapped in a conversation any longer. But it's also your responsibility to make sure you're not the one making someone else uncomfortable.

There may be times when the person you're conversing with wants to leave the dialogue, but you might not notice. The Meditator's Mindset tips for being present should help you to notice clues that you are not welcome and to act accordingly.

Consider the other person's body language. Are their arms open or crossed? Do they have a smile on their face or a scowl? Are they facing you directly or pointing away from you? Are they fully focused on you or are they fidgeting with their phone or something else, giving you only divided attention?

Just as each of these examples are actions that you now know to avoid when you want to build rapport, on the receiving end, they may be indicators that you are not welcome. Of course, you could be reading the signs incorrectly. If there is any doubt, simply ask, "Is it okay for me to speak with you now?" They will answer you honestly with either their words or their body language, and you can proceed from there.

If you are uncomfortable asking the above question, or if you get a sense that the other person is uncomfortable, then leave the situation and the person alone.

Someone might also openly tell you, "Please leave me alone." If this happens, then do as they say. Please don't pester people!

And remember, never comment on a person's body. I'm thin, just like my hair. I don't comment on other people's size, but when a friend or family member says, "Oh, you are so skinny. Are you eating enough?" I always get annoyed.

Speak Honestly, Not Offensively

It is also wise to avoid topics with high potential to offend. If a topic comes to mind and you hear the voice in your head question, *Is this subject okay to discuss now?* take that as a clue to keep it to yourself. It can be satisfying to speak about something that is a little shocking or newsworthy, but it might not be relevant or appropriate for the discussion. Perhaps that subject will be suitable to talk about with other familiar people, another time.

There is a delicate balance to find between speaking your mind spontaneously as soon as a thought surfaces and considering if what you say is going to be offensive. I totally support honest, spontaneous outbursts but only if they are not offensive. If people recoil at your comments, then you'll know you've gone too far. In this case, apologize. And then, use their feedback as information to learn just how much is safe to blurt out.

Diverse Perspectives

Keep in mind that it is easier for people with certain personalities to leave a conversation or any situation than it is for others. Gender plays a role too. My partner Renee says, "Whether I feel comfortable or not depends on the circumstances of the encounter and these questions often come to mind":

- How is this person approaching me?
- Is this a public or private place?
- Am I safe here?
- Are there people around?
- Does this person have another intention?
- Are they giving me space with their body language?
- Is this person hitting on me?

Renee also told me:

Sometimes I feel I have to smile to acknowledge that a man is there. It's a way to not agitate a possible attacker and to let them know that I can see them. Depending on the situation, I will either offer a really subtle smile (if I'm not interested in interaction) or a bigger smile if I feel safer and more open to communicating. I know that other women feel more comfortable avoiding eye contact altogether to avoid unwanted interactions. It is quite complicated because this small gesture of a smile can sometimes have larger consequences. Depending on how the smile is perceived by a man, it could invite more interaction than is wanted.

For the most part, if the person comes across as genuine, I feel safe to have that conversation. But I don't want to be rude, so even when they are talking their head off, I sometimes feel uncomfortable about leaving because I don't want to hurt them. So usually I wait for a lull or the end of the conversation to say, "Oh, okay, well, it was nice meeting you," and then I can move on. Creating an environment where everyone feels safe and respected is ideal for building a sense of connection.

Take Renee's perspective into consideration when you are speaking with someone. It is extremely important to consider if you are, in fact, welcome. If you aren't welcome, you could be doing harm and making them feel unsafe.

I'm not an expert in how much gender affects interactions between strangers, but it's important to know that there is a difference. It wasn't until I was in my forties that I learned that women tend to think about their physical safety much more often than men do. Having rarely felt threatened by other people, I've taken for granted the privilege of being a white, heterosexual man with full mobility who grew up in Canada.

There's so much negativity in the world that I've never experienced and, I'm embarrassed to say, I knew little about, until recently. I blame both the system I grew up in and myself for not becoming educated and aware at a younger age of the many social injustices facing marginalized groups in our country. I take responsibility for that. Now that the pandemic has brought to light many of these social injustices, it is up to us to educate ourselves, really dig in, and do the work to address and change them.

Uncomfortable Conversations
Need to Be Explored (Trigger Warning)

There could be a full book on uncomfortable conversations that need to be explored today. Knowing about social injustices and discussing them in a safe environment creates greater awareness and can lead to change.

Below is an incomplete reading list for increasing awareness about sexual harassment and abuse and the ongoing, systemic discrimination and mistreatment of Black, Indigenous, and people of colour (BIPOC) and people who identify as LGBTQQ2SIIAA+ (lesbian, gay, bisexual, transgender, queer, questioning, two-spirit, indigiqueer, intersex, asexual, ally, plus).

- Desmond Cole, *The Skin We're In: A Year of Black Resistance and Power* (Toronto: Doubleday Canada, 2020)

- Rodney Diverlus, Sandy Hudson, and Syrus Marcus Ware (editors), *Until We Are Free: Reflections on Black Lives Matter in Canada* (Regina, SK: University of Regina Press, 2020)

- Robyn Doolittle, *Had It Coming: What's Fair in the Age of #MeToo?* (New York: Allen Lane, 2019)

- Mason Funk, *The Book of Pride: LGBTQ Heroes Who Changed the World* (New York: HarperOne, 2019)

- Bob Joseph, *21 Things You May Not Know About the Indian Act: Helping Canadians Make Reconciliation with Indigenous Peoples a Reality* (Port Coquitlam, BC: Indigenous Relations Press, 2018)

- Jodi Kantor and Megan Twohey, *She Said: Breaking the Sexual Harassment Story That Helped Ignite a Movement* (New York: Penguin Press, 2019)

- Ibram X. Kendi, *How to Be an Antiracist* (London: One World, 2019)

- Thomas King, *An Inconvenient Indian: A Curious Account of Native People in North America* (Toronto: Anchor Canada, 2013)

- Justin Ling, *Missing from the Village: The Story of Serial Killer Bruce McArthur, the Search for Justice, and the System That Failed Toronto's Queer Community* (Toronto: McClelland & Stewart, 2020)

- Kai Cheng Thom, *I Hope We Choose Love: A Trans Girl's Notes from the End of the World* (Vancouver: Arsenal Pulp Press, 2019)

- Emmanuelle Walter, Susan Ouriou (translator), and Christelle Morelli (translator), *Stolen Sisters: The Story of Two Missing Girls, Their Families, and How Canada Has Failed Indigenous Women* (New York: HarperCollins, 2015)

How is it possible that diverse populations continue to experience harassment, discrimination, and such injustices today? These are uncomfortable conversations worth having to further educate us all and to create change. Greater awareness is a small first step to solving these challenging issues, so please take time to learn more. And if you see or hear someone saying something offensive or abusive, speak up!

At a rally that I attended in support of Indigenous people in Canada, one of the speakers said, "Canadians suffer from *obsessive civility*. They don't speak up when something is happening that they know is wrong because they are too damn polite!"

It is up to each of us to be vocal about what's right and wrong in our society today and to call it out. If we remain silent when incidents occur, then we are all guilty of maintaining the very social injustices that we need to resolve.

The last thing that I want is for anyone to feel uncomfortable when you use these techniques to connect with other people, so be mindful of your own and others' words and silences.

Listen

 Overcome
Internal Obstacles

 Open a Dialogue
—Six Strategies

 Keep (the Conversation)
Going

 Uncomfortable?
How to Exit a Conversation

 Play and Improvise

Play and Improvise

P: PLAY AND IMPROVISE

The noblest art is that of making others happy.
—*P.T. Barnum*

Today, with all of the seriousness that we must endure in our world, few techniques can be more effective in creating new connections than play. By being playful and lighthearted, you offer people a much-needed reprieve, and it is intriguing. While certain people are naturally more playful than others, anyone can use play to make new connections. Improvising is playful and can also help connect you to people. We will say yes to improv in this section as well.

Benefits of Play

The following benefits of play are reprinted with permission from https://helpguide.org/articles/mental-health/benefits-of-play-for-adults.htm. Play helps:

- *Relieve stress.* Play is fun and can trigger the release of endorphins, the body's natural feel-good chemicals. Endorphins promote an overall sense of well-being and can even temporarily relieve pain.

- *Improve brain function.* Playing chess, completing puzzles, or pursuing other fun activities that challenge the brain can help prevent memory problems and improve brain function. The social interaction of playing with family and friends can also help ward off stress and depression.

- *Stimulate the mind and boost creativity.* Young children often learn best when they are playing—a principle that applies to adults, as well. You'll learn a new task better when it's fun and you're in a relaxed and playful mood. Play can also stimulate your imagination, helping you to adapt and solve problems.

- *Improve relationships and your connection to others.* Sharing laughter and fun can foster empathy, compassion, trust, and intimacy with others. Play doesn't have to include a specific activity; it can also be a state of mind. Developing a playful nature can help you loosen up in stressful situations, break the ice with strangers, make new friends, and form new business relationships.

- *Keep you feeling young and energetic.* In the words of George Bernard Shaw, "We don't stop playing because we grow old; we grow old because we stop playing." Play can boost your energy and vitality and even improve your resistance to disease, helping you function at your best.

To these, I've added some specific benefits of being playful when meeting new people:

- If you feel comfortable enough to joke around with somebody you just met, it can be a great way to align with them. It's similar to mirroring with body language except in this case you match their level of joviality or playfulness. When you match up, you connect more deeply.

- Being playful in public is fun, and fun attracts more fun. It is similar to the "Invite a Compliment" strategy. When you are enjoying yourself with a group of friends, for example, things might get a little noisy. This attracts attention and others who want to play too.

- You get a chance to improve your sense of humour with no consequences. If you don't end up meeting a new person because your joke flopped, the timing was off, or they simply were not in the mood, it's okay. We are talking about complete strangers here. The stakes are low.

- You'll feel better looking because you'll smile more. And the act of smiling can improve your mood.[53]

- You become more approachable. Playful people are happy people. Of course, they are not happy all the time, but you can usually expect to see a smile on a playful person's face rather than a frown. When you are smiling, that positive body language will make strangers more receptive to having a conversation with you.

- You won't take yourself or others too seriously. Playful people don't care as much about what people think of them. They are less self-conscious. I have very few inhibitions, so I crack jokes and puns often. Having done this for more thirty years, I no longer fear what people think about me. I don't care. I've learned that it doesn't matter, and it's mostly positive anyhow.

- It is natural to assume that everybody cares what you say, do, and feel, but the truth is, for the most part, they don't. Most people are instinctively wrapped up in their own world, concerns, desires, fears, dreams, insecurities, challenges, and aspirations. They are too busy with their own life experience to pay much attention to yours. So if you dare to reach out to someone, and it doesn't go as hoped, it really doesn't matter. Life goes on.

- You empower others to have more fun in their lives. Playful people allow themselves to have fun. Everybody enjoys fun, but not everybody allows themselves to play. There is a difference. You can be a role model to others. Being playful gives others permission that they sometimes need to relax and open up as well.

- Being playful can even save you money! I once saved $50 on a windshield replacement while pretending that it was my birthday, then joking around about how it was not. I asked, "May I still have the birthday discount?" And the receptionist said, "We don't offer any discount for birthdays, but that was fun, so you're getting a deal."

With these benefits available to you, how can you afford not to play more? If you think of play as an investment in your future, this might help motivate you to give it a try. And your work can even turn into play. This was my experience when I joined the circus.

Consider how you can treat yourself sometime within the next month to an activity that you truly want to have in your life. Schedule it.

"I Don't Have Time to Play!"

If you lead a high-octane lifestyle with family, work, or other responsibilities that leave little to no time for you to enjoy yourself, it may be difficult to unwind. And play may not seem like a worthwhile option for you. But there are dangerous potential consequences to play deprivation.[54] Consider becoming a little more playful for pleasure and your wellness.

You may have valid reasons for being unable to do the activities that you want to do: lack of time, overwork, financial restrictions, or caring of others (partner, kids, parents, unexpected vagabond house guests, exotic pets, etc.). Despite those reasons, consider how you can treat yourself sometime within the next month to an activity that you truly want to have in your life. Schedule time for yourself. You deserve it.

Now, this doesn't mean that you'll have to do the activity by yourself. It may very well include other people. But the important thing is to schedule it. If you don't, the connections you could have made while doing something that you love to do—like the one described below—may never happen.

A close friend, Allen Porayko, had been offering to take me rock climbing for about a year. This was something that I dearly wanted to do, but I always said no. I would always complain that work—which I wasn't even happy with—was too busy. But at a deep level back then, I didn't believe I deserved to do activities that I wanted to do, so I made excuses.

But sometimes the timing can be so sweet.

When Al finally got me to the gym in December 2011, he introduced me to his climbing partner, Ian. We had met a couple of times before but never really chatted. At the time, Ian was completing his master's degree at SUNY Buffalo State College in creative studies. While climbing, we spoke about my desire to make a career change into professional presenting.

"Would you like to learn a few things about creativity?" he asked.

"Sure," I said.

"I've got some really cool tools that I'd like to try out and that you could benefit from."

"Sounds good." I was excited.

To begin, he led me through the FourSight Breakthrough Thinking Profile and I learned that I am an Ideator-Implementer.[55]

This led to other insightful meetings. Ian was very generous with his resources and I greatly enjoyed the creativity exercises. He suggested I attend an event called MoMondays. Then on May 7, 2012, I delivered a short talk on my European adventures.

The most engaging and experienced presenter that evening was Tim Hurson. I will never forget when we met at the end of the event. He firmly shook my hand, looked me intently in the eyes, and told me, "You're coming to Mindcamp, right?" I was a little surprised by such a confident invitation to which I could only reply, "Yes."

So that August, at my first creativity conference, Mindcamp, I delivered a "night-flight"—an informal evening presentation—using juggling to teach focus. Tim is one of the founders and warmly welcomed me to the community.

The conference was fantastic for a number of reasons. It took place in a beautiful natural setting; I learned a great deal about creativity; I met more wonderful people; and I had a ton of fun. Unbeknownst to me at the time, I had been introduced to a colourful new world of experiences that would have a profound impact on my life.

A new friend I met that week, Francois Coetzee from South Africa, attended my session and connected with me after the conference. He encouraged me to apply to deliver the session at the upcoming ACRE Creativity Conference. To my absolute delight, it was accepted and just five weeks later, I went to South Africa. I delivered the closing keynote there, a session with the Springboks (the national rugby sevens team) and got to work with a youth group on top of Table Mountain. Early in my career as a presenter, this was encouraging and exciting.

But how did this adventure find me?

It found me because I made time to do something for myself—to play— despite feeling overwhelmed with work.

I have now participated in ten creativity conferences and have become a part of a global creativity community that continues to enrich my life today.

Looking back, I can reflect on how important and timely it was for me to meet Ian. The creative processes that he led me through are the reason I was finally able to quit the toxic job that I had felt stuck in for over three years. As soon as I accepted that I deserved better and that I deserved to play, my life improved through this chain of events. If you would like to experience the world of creativity, visit the Other Resources section to find out how.

Incredibly, this all started with a conversation. It began with me saying yes to doing something that I really wanted as a part of my life. It is very much the same with improv, which we will get to shortly.

You can say yes to play too.

"But how can I be playful if I'm not a playful person?" you might ask. Here are some tips for bringing the spirit of play into your conversations.

How to Use Play to Connect with People

Bring Your Inner Child Back to Life

As we grow up and are groomed for the "real world," we can lose that sense of play we once had as children. We are taught to not express things that are out of the ordinary—to not use our voices. In a sense, we're taught to not be our playful selves. And most of us adults just forget how to be playful and were never told how good and even necessary it is for our well-being. So, if you need a refresher, here it is:

Let's resuscitate that little playful inner soul. Remember that the Child's Mindset requires you to be spontaneous and curious. And the Juggler's Mindset requires that you be adventurous. These are all playful characteristics. It is time to express yourself and do the playful things you didn't think twice about when you were young.

By being playful, you create magical moments for other adults to feel that they have permission to be playful too. This is a glorious gift for many people who rarely expose themselves to fun. It can lead to a real shift.

Notice and Share What Amuses You

Make use of your incredible senses. Drop the devices. Look up and see what's going on in your surroundings. In a relaxed state, allow yourself to notice what amuses and entertains you, no matter how big or small. When something amuses you, let someone know. These observations can become shortcuts to you blurting something funny out loud. These can also be entertaining talking points with strangers. You might share what happened and your reaction with the person next to you, or you might mention it to the person who just spilled the soup, made a great joke, farted, got mud on their face, slid on the ice, dropped their ice cream cone—fill in the blank. When you courageously express how something entertained you, the person next to you (who is likely a witness or the cause) will almost certainly celebrate this moment with you. Even if you or they are embarrassed! This is another example of triangulation, which was mentioned in the "Open a Dialogue" chapter.

Here's an example of me adding a little humour after a serious situation during my Talk2MorePeople challenge:

T2MP Day 351

While paying for a therapy session at the Calgary Counselling Centre, I joked with the cashier, "I would like to pay my fine here." We both had a chuckle, which I needed after an intense conversation. Moments later, in the elevator,

122

a man who had overheard me joking around said, "Hey, what you said then made me laugh." That is how I met Alejandro. I asked him, "Where is your accent from?" and he said he was from Colombia. This started an enjoyable conversation. When you joke around with people, you give others the permission they sometimes need to relax and open up. This can work even in a serious setting, as long as you keep your joke or comment respectful.

Spend More Time with Playful People

Even if you don't personally know playful people, there probably are playful people you have access to. They could be friends of friends, family members, or colleagues. When you see people having a good time, it's natural to want to be a part of it, so why not ask if you can join in? Say, "It looks like you are having a great time. May I join you?" If you always wait for an invitation before joining the fun, you can miss out on a lot of parties, events, and celebrations. Have you ever crashed a party or a wedding? I've done so a handful of times and have always been warmly welcomed. Remember the wise words of my mother: "The squeaky wheel gets the grease."

Get in the Game

Perhaps you'd feel more comfortable asking to join a game than joke around with others. That works too. Groups of people who actually play a game together will bring more play into your life, but only if you approach them.

More than ten years ago in Toronto, I simply asked to join people who were throwing the Frisbee around and met an entire friend group who remain close friends to this day. When they needed a substitute, I was invited to join their Ultimate Frisbee team.

Stand by and observe a game in progress. Take a breath and ask someone on the sidelines, "Hey, can I sub in?" and watch your community expand. You can use this with beach volleyball, Ultimate Frisbee, or pickup basketball, for example. Go ahead. Get in the game! You never know. You just might become the next captain.

Don't Put Too Much Pressure on Yourself to Be Funny

Talented comedians are experts at connecting thoughts and words quickly. They rehearse and deliver jokes to entertain audiences. It is an extremely challenging art form in which the artist makes use of current events, their life experience, or anything they can think up to create an entertaining world during their performances.

Friend, fellow performer, comedian, and self-described musical clown Braden Lyster (aka Troo Knot) had this to say when I asked him how to use comedy to connect with people.

Before going on stage to do music or comedy I remind myself not to worry about performing and just focus on having fun. Funny usually comes from a playful state so focus on feeling light and open. What's the point of performing, meeting new people, or going on dates if we're stressing about our performance the entire time? Be honest, be silly, be playful, and enjoy the ride. Everyone has their own quirky brand of funny, so just have fun being you and people will often connect with that feeling. And know that if you make a bad joke and no one laughs, they are probably laughing at you on the inside... which still counts.

Join As If You Are Already In

This is a more advanced playfulness strategy. As you become more comfortable with joking around, you will be able to chime in on the fly and be comfortable acting as if you're already part of the conversation. Of course, it doesn't work all the time, but when it does, it's as if you are subbing in as a new player on your favourite team. Boom! It's game on. You join the interaction.

T2MP Day 358

On my way out of the Kahanoff Centre today, I heard the two security guards, Bob and Kathy, ask John at reception, "So what's new?" When I overheard this, I approached them and asked, "May I tell you what's new for me?" They warmly received me and I told them, "I am about to meet a completely new stranger today and have a conversation about something random." And with this, we all got into a nice exchange.

In the above example, I wasn't out hunting for a conversation; rather, I stumbled upon it. I acted as if I was already in the conversation from the beginning. Opportunities to join conversations may come up much more easily than you'd expect, now that you are listening for them.

You can also eventually get to a point, if you play with it enough, when it becomes automatic. It will eventually just happen. For many, this is already naturally the case. You may now know people who engage with strangers regularly when they hear something they can relate to. And then you witness the beautiful exchange of spontaneous stories and see them create new connections all the time. Perhaps you've felt envious and thought, Wow. I wish I could do that. Hang in there, soon you will be able to.

If you're too nervous to try this right off the bat, you might ease into it by spending time with playful people and learning from them, watching comedy for inspiration, or joking around with people you know before trying it with a random stranger.

Be Authentic

Be real with others and yourself when you use humour in public. Make jokes that are within range for your personality. It's fantastic to stretch beyond your comfort zone to create humour as long as you are still being true to yourself. Authenticity creates the best jokes of all.

Joke to Raise People Up, Not Put Them Down

Avoid making jokes at the expense of someone else. This might occasionally be okay with siblings or close friends, but definitely avoid such jokes with strangers. A little self-deprecating humour is one exception that can work well to break the ice sometimes. Just don't use this technique too much because then it's not a good time. Better yet, why not tell a joke that raises another person up in a positive light? The results from this will be much more favourable.

Give a Joke, Take a Joke

While humour is a wonderful way to build connections, it has to be a two-way street. Make sure that you can laugh at yourself if the joke's on you. Don't dish it out if you can't take it.

Beware the Sting of Sarcasm

Perhaps you are a sarcastic person with your friends and colleagues. Maybe it's not your fault. You might be from England. While sarcasm can be funny, it can cause unspoken resentment or agitation. The problem is that it often leads to a put-down. There is a certain amount of truth in humour, so be cautious how you use sarcasm. Use it only with people you know well enough that they will actually tell you to sod off if you've upset them.

Use the Power of Puns

The dictionary defines *pun* as "a humorous use of a word or phrase that has several meanings or that sounds like another word." They often make people laugh or groan in agony as if you stole their oxygen.

"Puns are the lowest form of humour," teachers always told me. "Well then, why is everybody laughing?" I would reply. As a high school student, I remember getting kicked out of class a couple of times for making puns. I don't remember any serious consequences for such offences, but as an adult, puns have helped me meet people. Puns can help you meet people too.

Puns are witty. You need to think on your feet and dare to speak up if you are going to use them. People will say that they are "pun-ishment" to listen to. When I drop a particularly awful one, my mother still says to this day that I "o-punned the door." Of course, not everyone is going to appreciate your quip. But the majority of the time, you will create original moments when connecting with someone new (even if, in fact, the moment or joke wasn't that funny). When someone gives you their chair, for example, you can say, "That was very 'chair-itable' of you."

Works every *time*, as long as I *watch* the situation. Oh, do you need a *hand* with that last one? Didn't mean to *alarm* you with these puns that just arrived on *time*.

Don't wait for permission when a funny quip comes to mind; just say it out loud. You likely won't get kicked out of class for it, especially if you are no longer a student. Here's a story of when I used a pun to start a conversation.

T2MP Day 332

In the physiotherapy waiting room, I had a chance to work on my phone but stopped myself. Instead, I put the phone away.

As I put my jacket on the coat rack, I said, "I'm going to be like this jacket and hang out for a while." Joelle and her daughter, who were also waiting, laughed, and the three of us had a conversation.

Over the course of our dialogue, I shared that I once spent half an hour in a "pun-off" competition while hiking on the Great Wall of China with my good friend and fellow punster Will Henry. Back then, the wall was trembling beneath our feet in disdain as we hiked.

Our waiting room conversation then evolved into a deeper discussion about the importance of listening to one another. It was a fun exchange of laughter followed by new insights that started because of a pun.

In those few minutes I could have caught up on a few emails or writing, but I know that I made the right choice to co-create this conversation with a little humour.

There are many ways to use humour to break the ice with people. Even if it's not your normal style to tell jokes, give it a try.

Improvise

There are several delightful ways to play. A fantastic group activity to watch, learn, or participate in is improvised theatre, also known as "improv." Improvisers make the scenes up on the spot, without a script. When done properly, this leads to great comedy. You can do this too.

Learning improv has many benefits. It helps you to use your voice, become more confident, read body language, and appropriately give and receive offers within a scene. It teaches people who might have previously been closed-minded to say, "Yes, and...", and of course, it is great fun. I was very fortunate to have studied improv at The Second City Training Centre in Toronto, Canada. Years later, it helped me meet people on the Talk2MorePeople Project and led to many nights of play and laughter with strangers and new friends. Here's how that unfolded.

T2MP Day 220

On this day, I met Mike Wilkes. He had written about the Talk2MorePeople Project in his blog after reading a CBC article about it.[56] *We were introduced online through a mutual contact in Toronto, Chris Snoyer. Mike and I met in person and hit it off over beers. He mentioned that he wanted to try improv. I had been wanting to host improv events for a while. I told Mike, "If you agree to come, I'll host an improv jam next week." He replied, "I'll be there."*

I hosted and a half-dozen people, including Mike, showed up for an informal evening of improv. This marked the beginning of many evenings of play with all kinds of people. The conversation with Mike led to real-world events where more people made new connections. It created that ripple effect of positivity. This is how random conversations can change lives.

But I'm not an improviser, you may be thinking. *I don't have any training.*

If you have lived long enough to read these words, you have improvised countless times in your life already. Not for a performance necessarily, but for survival. Daily, there are situations when you are forced to think on your feet, to say yes to the situational parameters, and to make a choice without knowing what the outcome will be.

Here are some possible examples from your life:

- When your sibling took all the Lego, and instead of crying about it, you built an epic fort out of blankets or pillows, you improvised.

- When you were out so late you had to break into your childhood home so your parents wouldn't hear you come in the front door, you improvised.

- When you cooked a random splodge (unidentified stew) for your family with the remaining ingredients in your fridge, you improvised.

- When you wrote someone's phone number on your arm because you didn't have paper or a napkin, you improvised (pre-smartphones).

- When you fixed something on your car, bike, boat, toy, or castle with duct tape, you improvised.

Improvising a conversation relates to the examples above because, essentially, you need to make do with what is available to you at the time. Human brains are pretty smart and are always making connections, so you may think that you are not an improviser, but, in fact, you are.

By improvising a conversation, we landed the exact job we wanted on the same day that we landed in that country. Imagine the possibilities within reach for you.

Say "Yes, and…"

The most fundamental component of improv is to say "yes, and…" "Yes" to whatever offer your fellow improviser provides; "and" means that you add something to what was just offered. It is about being open to the offer that comes to you on stage and going with it, no matter what it is. You build ideas and scenes together. People do this while in conversations as well.

A Talk2MorePeople encounter is very similar because you never know what you are going to get when you approach a stranger. Talking with strangers on a regular basis helps break down preconceived notions and judgments about what a person is going to be like based on their appearance. Say "yes" and be open to what they have to say, "and" then make your own contribution. Once an interaction has been sparked, each person involved needs to be somewhat of an improviser to keep the interaction going. And this will be no problem for you as you have now seen how you've been improvising all your life.

Live on stage or in conversation with new people, there are no perfect scripts that will give you the same results every time. We often can't control the direction of the conversation. In improv, we often can't control the direction of a scene. And that's the beauty of it! The natural, random spontaneity allows for magic moments to manifest. That's why the Juggler's Mindset is so important. If you can be adaptable, you can handle just about anything.

If you can become okay with improvising, you will enjoy feeling more relaxed and better prepared for the unexpected twists and turns that life throws your way. Here's a story about how a willingness to be adaptable and improvise led to a great opportunity.

On my twenty-sixth birthday, I flew from Toronto to Brazil with my partner. After my year and a half in Europe, I wanted to study Portuguese so that I could speak with my father in his first language. At the time, I could only understand a few swear words that I had learned on job sites. The way to learn Portuguese, I thought, was to move to Brazil and teach English.

Upon arrival, we checked into a hostel and spoke with the man at reception whose English was fluent. It was like any other standard tourist conversation you would expect with normal questions like "Where are you from?" and "How long are you travelling?"

But eventually he asked, "Why are you visiting Brazil?"

"We are looking for jobs teaching English," we replied.

"Oh, my girlfriend runs an English school and is looking for teachers now. You will have to meet her."

This exciting news caught us by surprise. Of course, even though we were exhausted from our twelve-hour flight, we continued to speak with him to learn more about the opportunity. By taking what was offered to us in that discussion, we improvised a conversation.

Two days later, we were hired for our first teaching jobs in Brazil in the city of Guaratinguetá. We went with the flow of the unexpected conversation. Later, we moved to a city in the south called Florianópolis, which is a coastal beach-town paradise. By improvising a conversation with this man, we landed the exact job we wanted on the same day that we landed in that country. Imagine the possibilities within reach for you. You don't need to be travelling for this to happen. You only need to be open to a little improvisation and to being adaptable.

Consider taking an improv course or joining an improv jam in your community. The improv will improve your life and be piles of fun.

Take lessons from the improvisers you observe or the one that you become to be present, spontaneous, curious, adventurous, and adaptable. Finally, say "yes, and..." to opportunities to connect with people.[57]

It's Okay If They Don't Want to Play

Using improv, making a joke, or being playful in public happens when you take a risk. But what if people don't like the joke? What if you look silly? Will people give you strange looks? Does it matter?

In childhood, you likely couldn't play with everyone. There were kids you got along with and those you didn't. It's the same for us as adults. Not everyone will want to play all the time. Keep in mind that that's totally normal and don't let it discourage you. By being playful, you will likely accomplish at least one thing: you will entertain yourself. When you reach out to create a conversation or connection with another person, they almost always positively respond because you are doing something generative. But if they don't, it doesn't mean that there is anything wrong with you or with the other person. Embrace a spirit of playfulness even in failure by not taking it too seriously.

Deep down, everyone likes to play sometimes, even miserable-looking people. They just try to not let you see it. Do you remember Ebenezer Scrooge from *A Christmas Carol*? For almost the entire story he was miserable and grouchy. A humbug. But in the end, after spending time with the Ghosts of Christmas Past, Present, and Future, he was dancing and laughing and making jokes. It is possible to shift into a playful space, and you don't need to wait for old age or to see ghosts for it to happen. It is a choice.

You May Receive Strange Looks, and It Doesn't Matter

Indeed, a few people won't allow themselves to loosen up at all. There will be times when you do something playful in public and receive a certain look from a stranger. It could appear to be confusion—that sort of Mona Lisa half-smile look of uncertainty. That's the look of a person who wants to be playful but, for whatever reason, doesn't think that they can be.

While it is unfortunate that not everyone who could become playful in a situation will choose to do so, you will still have made a positive impression with your playfulness. They saw you have fun or make (good, clean) fun of a situation or yourself, and that will have affected that person. Perhaps the next time they are in a situation like this, they will engage. You may have helped move the needle on their level of playfulness by facilitating fun.

Being playful is not only about the people you interact with. Of course, it's also about you! If you expressed yourself in a moment of playfulness, then you did something good. And by doing this good thing, you created the possibility that you could more easily connect with a stranger, which is progress for your social development. Well done! Keep in mind that it's also okay to just play for the sake of having fun.

Play Deepens Existing Connections

When you are playful in public with strangers, it can only serve you positively because they can't compare you against any previous version of yourself. This really boils down to the fact that it just doesn't matter what people think. When you are playful with people you already know, it can deepen existing connections.

If you are not known as a playful person but you start acting more playful around family and friends, they will be pleasantly surprised. By doing something out of character that is fun, your people will notice and this can by itself lead to deeper connections because you're showing a new, fun side of yourself. That's a form of vulnerability that helps build human connection.

All of this business of meeting new people is risky, but so is life. But what is the greater risk? Approaching strangers and, maybe, occasionally getting rejected? Or not approaching new people and living a life of isolation? And haven't we all experienced enough isolation already because of the global pandemic? The extent of the damaging effects from such isolation won't be known for years.

For a list of fun and somewhat ridiculous things that I do to bring more play into my life, visit the Other Resources section at the end of the book.

CONCLUSION

So now that you have had an in-depth look at the LOOKUP Process for Meeting People, what do you think? Did you discover something in there that you'll use on your journey of human connection? Does it seem far-fetched or totally possible to meet new people now? Have you tried yet? Have you experienced an information gift exchange already?

Whatever you got from this so far is okay, as long as you use at least part of it.

There has been an epidemic of loneliness on the planet for years now. So by reaching out to another person, by using anything that you have learned on your own or with this book, you are doing a service. You are helping alleviate the loneliness that millions of people suffer from.[58] It doesn't even matter if the conversation itself is a total flop, because you will have impacted that person by interacting with them. So disregard any thoughts that you might have had in the past that you are inconveniencing someone by interrupting them or that you are being a bother by attempting to strike up a conversation. You are doing a good thing even if, at times, nothing comes of it.

Can you think of a shared experience that you could use to connect with a neighbour today?

But chances are that something *great* will happen as a result of your efforts. You may even strike up a new business relationship or friendship with someone you meet. People don't need to know each other for years to become close friends. If two strangers can become friends after spending forty-one days together on an unexpected bike trip, it can happen in your day-to-day life too.

It happens with travellers all the time. Two people from different cultures arrive at a youth hostel in Southeast Asia with no plans for the evening. They easily get into a conversation as they share common ground: the experience of travelling. There are so many topics to effortlessly discuss while on the road. "Where are you from? How long have you been moving? What's great to do nearby? How is life in your country?" This conversation by proximity leads to an evening of adventure and before you know it, they become friends for life.

How is it possible for people to become such good friends so quickly? When you are in the same place as another person who is having the same experience, often you have a natural desire to share it, whether you're home or abroad, spending days or hours together or even a few minutes. You only need to share an experience with another person.

Can you think of a shared experience that you could use to connect with a neighbour today? Embrace the Traveller's Mindset, and you may find that connecting with people in your hometown becomes much more natural.

So it may, in fact, be easier than you think to build rapport or to connect with other people. But you never know if you never put yourself out there!

Gillian Sandstrom and Erica J. Boothby's 2020 study "Why Do People Avoid Talking to Strangers?" proves that our fears of speaking to strangers are unjustified:

> We meta-analyzed seven studies to examine the fears that people have about talking to strangers. People's worries about not enjoying the conversation, not liking their partner, and not being able to carry out the conversation, as well as their worries about their partner not enjoying the conversation, not liking them, and not being able to carry out the conversation were all inter-correlated, and related to actual talking behaviour. A comparison of pre-conversation predictions to post-conversation experiences revealed that all of people's fears were vastly overblown.[59]

People worry much more than they should when approaching strangers. But you don't need to any longer.

You've been learning different tools to meet new people and playing with them in public. Perhaps you have made new contacts, found a new job, or just enjoyed learning this is a skill that is possible to learn. What's next?

To wrap things up, in this conclusion you will find a new challenge and a few more stories. Following the conclusion are success stories from other people to put a little more pep into your step.

Take the Talk2MorePeople 30-Day Challenge

If you've started experimenting with the tips in this book and feel like you're ready to push yourself further, great! Try this life-changing 30-Day Challenge.

Do you appreciate a challenge or does it make you shy away or want to simply turn the page? A good challenge can stretch you, be difficult, or be frustrating, but it can also help you focus and grow. Whether you like challenges or not, this one was an important part of the Talk2MorePeople Project, and it can change your life for the better. It is here for you to explore now.

In April 2016, I began to document the outcomes from intentionally meeting a new stranger every day for thirty days. Having achieved more from taking other 30-Day Challenges than I thought possible, I expected to experience positive results. I completed 30DaysofWriting, Last30Daysof30s (a daily video-creation challenge), 30DaysofPushUps, and 30DaysofMeditation.[60] Each of these yielded positive results.

In my case, the journey of meeting strangers extended to 365 days, but let's take a more detailed look at the 30-Day Challenge that started it all.

What Is a 30-Day Challenge?

It is an opportunity for you to either do or not do something every day for thirty days. This makes a potentially overwhelming task possible because you know that it has an end date. A 30-Day Challenge is usually very personal, requires a substantial amount of effort, and can be very motivating.

What Are the Benefits?

The benefits vary greatly depending on the type of challenge that you undertake, but they will often include the following:

- Improved self-discipline
- Greater results than expected
- A meaningful reason to get out of bed every day
- A sense of accomplishment
- Improved mental health
- Connection to an existing community
- Personal and/or professional growth

How to Complete a 30-Day Challenge

There are four main steps to take to complete a 30-Day Challenge:

1. Set a reasonable goal for yourself. If it is too large, you may become overwhelmed quickly and quit. It should be manageable and possible.

2. Decide to create the time to do the task every day for thirty days. It can be helpful to set a reminder or schedule it into your day.[61]

3. Make the challenge a priority over other events. "If you are saying yes to this, what are you saying no to?" This is the Strategic Question in *The Coaching Habit* by Michael Bungay Stanier.

4. Keep going until completion despite the inevitable resistance. Allow yourself to experience the benefits of your efforts.

Your Positive Mindset

The most important aspect of completing such a challenge is mindset. You are capable of doing whatever you believe you can accomplish. If you go into a challenge with a positive mindset, there is a good chance that you will accomplish it or at least achieve positive results. Having doubt is normal. But if the doubt is overwhelming and causing physical or emotional stress, then you might not be able to complete your goal. And that's okay. Just move the goalposts. In this case, you may have set a goal that is unreasonable for you. This does not mean that you can't ever accomplish that goal, but maybe now is not the right time. You can improve your mindset by practising Tracey's mindfulness techniques in the Appendix.

One More Tool to Help You

While intentionally meeting someone new every day for a year, I would often give them my business card, which had an open calendar on the back of it. That was the Talk2MorePeople 30-Day Challenge. I referred to it as a business card with a "life-changing challenge" because when you meet new people, your life changes—usually for the better. The offer was for people to tick a box every day that they met someone new.[62] Pull your cards out of the back of this book or visit Talk2MorePeople.com/tools for your free download.

You can use the card as a prop to get into conversations. To do so, take the card out and, while holding it, turn to a person you would like to speak with. Be sure this person is stationary and not on the move or walking in the opposite direction from you.

With the card in your hand and a smile on your face, say, "Excuse me, may I ask you a quick question? I've been given a challenge to meet new people this month. It's part of this concept called Talk2MorePeople (show them the card). May I speak with you for a minute?"

They will likely agree. Congratulations—you just met someone! Then make use of the LOOKUP Process that you've been learning, breathe through it, and have fun.

My wish in giving out this card was that dozens of people would complete it and share their life-changing encounters. After all, every person who was offered the card accepted it. I gave out hundreds of these things, and there were zero rejections. Many people were visibly excited about the idea, and some reported back to me that they were either attempting the challenge or had completed it. I felt so passionately about the great results I had experienced that I expected people would jump at the chance to meet new people and encourage others to do so as well. I wanted it to create more face-to-face interactions and a ripple effect of positivity.

What is the ripple effect that you want to create in this world?

But what I was hoping for didn't exactly happen. At least, not in the way I expected it to.

Although several individuals completed the challenge and told others about it, thirty days is too big of an ask for many people. Despite this, as the project went on, I kept on giving out the 30-Day Challenge cards.

One result from giving out these cards was that it created conversations on the importance of face-to-face conversations. I received emails and messages from people telling me this. Those conversations often happened without me being involved, so new people were learning about the idea and discussing in-person connections. And although individuals were not necessarily ticking the boxes on the card every day, they were still interacting with the concept and learning more about the subject. That made, and continues to make, a positive impact.

137

So, upon reflection, these efforts *had* created a ripple effect—it just wasn't what I expected when starting out. The card is not only a physical tool you can use as a prop and a record but one final lesson about perseverance even when the results aren't what you expect. Now that this book is in your hands, the ripple has an opportunity to expand further. Words and the human connection are like waves. A drop in the ocean can create movement great distances away. What is the ripple effect that you want to create in this world?

What If I Miss a Day?

Have you slipped and missed a day with a challenge? If so, how much easier was it to miss the next day? If you missed two days in a row, did you give up completely?

When we drop the ball with a challenge, we can lose momentum. It is as if we give ourselves permission to skip the next day, or even throw in the towel completely, because we already screwed up and feel like we've failed. And that misstep becomes the excuse that we use to really own that failure and to not continue the challenge. Don't let this happen to you. Remember that dropping the ball is an essential part of learning how to juggle. What is also required with juggling is picking the ball back up. We can learn a lesson from this art form as it relates to the worthy challenge of meeting new people every day for a month.

Giving up if you miss a day is a premature reaction after putting in so much effort. Think about it. You decided to do something that is important to you every day for some amount of time, and then you started to do that thing! That task may have been something that you were avoiding for months or even years. Starting was already a huge and courageous accomplishment, so don't throw it all away.

While it is not ideal, it is totally normal to miss a day in a challenge. We are human, not perfect. That's part of what makes us so beautiful. But when/if it does happen, there is a new challenge—and that is not to restart but rather to pick up where you left off the very next day. Doing so may be even more difficult than getting the courage to start in the first place. But now you have the energy of having started that thing behind you for support.

If you miss a day, so what? Don't quit completely. Keep going. Pick up the ball.

You may feel pressure from a peer or within yourself to start all over again to get it perfect, but that is a dangerous mistake. It is a better idea to continue the next day from where you left off because you might get too discouraged to restart. After all, I missed Day 79 and continued to complete the Talk2MorePeople Project. This led to profoundly positive results for me, even though I didn't do it perfectly.

You have a greater chance of getting results from a challenge completed imperfectly than from one that just stopped. And what do we all want most out of a challenge? Results.

When it comes to the Talk2MorePeople 30-Day Challenge, done is better than perfect. This challenge provides an opportunity to get positive results even if you slip up. It allows you to keep going. Are you going to think like an improviser and say "yes, and" to this opportunity?

The greatest takeaway is not only that most people are actually happy to talk to strangers, but also that there is so much to learn and explore through these conversations.

If you are reading this now and thinking, *Yeah, this sounds great, but I could never do that,* it probably means you should make an attempt at it. Uncomfortable moments or thoughts like this are clear opportunities for learning and growth.

But I'll let you off the hook. If the 30-Day Challenge is not for you, don't sweat it. There is another option. Put in 10 percent of the effort, and you will still likely get positive results. That means that you only need to go out of your way to meet three new people in the next month, rather than thirty. You will also need to be open to discomfort and to the positive possibilities that it can create. Use the card. Use the LOOKUP Process. Use whatever works for you.

Results

What results can you expect from taking on this challenge? As is true for many things, what you put into it is what you'll get out of it. So why not aim high and expect phenomenal results? But be ready to work or play (depending on your preference) towards them as the results won't magically appear on their own.

In my case, I was very fortunate. The results from intentionally meeting strangers were hands-and-feet-down transformational. These new relationships created a considerable upgrade to the overall quality of my life in every area. Towards the end of my challenge, it really started to sink in:

T2MP Day 313

I met Marnie and Laura one Sunday afternoon at Mikey's Juke Joint while listening to excellent live music by Ben and Chuck Rose. While I was speaking with them, Marnie asked me, "What has been the greatest takeaway so far from this project?" I paused because there have been so many benefits that it seemed like an overwhelming question.

But the first thing that came to me was, "The realization that people actually really do want to talk to strangers. It often seems like they don't, but that's not actually the case. Day after day after day of approaching people (whether I was in the mood to or not), people have been happy to share time and conversation. And a majority of these conversations have been rich with new information and ideas that I've been able to explore. So I guess that means that the greatest takeaway is not only that most people are actually happy to talk to strangers, but also that there is so much to learn and explore through these conversations."

It is as if we are constantly surrounded by everything that we could ever need or want to know. And to access this, we just need to break the ice with the people who surround us. Laura and Marnie also shared their experiences talking to strangers.

Laura shared, "I was out for breakfast yesterday morning. An older man started speaking to me and offered me a candy. And it was my favourite kind! Then he asked if he could have breakfast with me and I happily agreed." She added, "I loved speaking to this older man because he reminded me of my late father. 'I was so impressed to learn that I'm not the only one who would spontaneously have a meal with a complete stranger,' he said."

Marnie chimed in, "I have no problems talking to people. There are too many missed opportunities... When I meet people, I need to share myself with them and also I need to learn from them. And I'm going to do more of that." I gave her the 30-Day Challenge and guaranteed that if she takes on the challenge, amazing things will happen. She seemed keen to take it on. (And she completed it.)

One question that Marnie asked me was, "What is the biggest type of change in your life since doing this project?" I told her, "There's an awful lot more live music in my life now. That's wonderful. Also, I have a number of new, important friends in my life, including my friend Tru, who is sitting next to me now.

"We have this illusion that everybody is plugged into technology and would rather not interact, but that's not actually the case. Being buried in the smartphone seems like a safe hiding place for many of us, but I have discovered through this journey that that's actually not where people prefer to be. How we use and interact with today's addictive technology is a very important topic that needs to be discussed to be better understood and managed.

"When you interrupt someone and you take the initiative, when you interact, almost all people are interested and willing to have a conversation and explore the possibilities within it."

My wish is that this exploration of the human connection has helped you fall more in love with people so that you can more effectively live your life on your own terms.

Along with the many other benefits I've shared in the stories throughout this book, the Talk2MorePeople Project introduced me to my partner, Renee. Here's one last success story from me:

T2MP Day 305

Two new friends, Tru and Ryan, whom I met on Day 142 and Day 258 of the project, had invited me to a house concert/potluck outside of Calgary. They were performing that night. I was on the fence about attending because I didn't have a car. It was going to take effort to get there. You know those times when you feel that it would be best to go to an event but you just want to be lazy? Despite that, I decided at the last minute to go.

Am I ever pleased that I did!

At the beginning of the evening, I sat next to a young woman during the opening meditation. I felt an immediate attraction to her. There had been no romance in the past nine months of my life despite meeting so many fantastic people, so I was feeling extra awkward.

Because I was in the habit of approaching new people and had developed methods for comfortably doing so, I was able to strike up a conversation. It was almost as if I was on autopilot meeting people, so despite my anxiety at that time, I was able to approach her. Acting on impulse, I went over during the break, when food was out for people to share and enjoy, and I asked the first question that came to mind. "How are you enjoying the food?"

"It's good, thanks," she replied. "How about you?"

With that, we broke the ice, my anxiety reduced, and a conversation developed that seemed to flow reasonably well. Renee had seen me present at an event nine months earlier, but this was the first time we had properly met. I was able to tame my enthusiasm and not scare her away, and we agreed to get in touch after the event.

A couple of weeks later, we made a meal together, went out, and hit it off. Then we went hiking. Then we had more meals together, laughed a lot, and became partners. We have lived life to the fullest together ever since. Our mutual love for nature has had us explore Alberta's and British Columbia's beautiful mountains through countless adventures. We share the same passions for travel, living sustainably, eating healthy food, and playing together. It has been four years of love and joy since we met, and I think we've got about seventy-eight years left.

I went from living in chronic bachelorhood for several years to experiencing the comfort of a loving, supportive, exciting relationship that continues to bring growth and joy into my life today.

If you wait until circumstances are perfect before you take a leap of faith, you may never jump. And then you never get to fly.

There were times when I dreamt that I might meet my life partner on this journey, but it was never an expectation. That it happened, I believe, is either just good fortune or good statistics. If you meet more people, then more opportunities come your way. It's pretty simple math.

Have you heard the phrase, "You must love yourself before anyone else can love you"? Although I see the logic in that, I didn't love myself when I met Renee. I was in a dark place and was questioning everything. I was frustrated to be still trying to figure my life out—despite professional help— at the age of forty-two, yet somehow she and I connected. If you wait until circumstances are perfect before you take a leap of faith, you may never jump. And then you never get to fly.

I sincerely hope that you're inspired to play with the tools, techniques and process in this book to create new connections and opportunities in your own life.

Now we are reaching the end of this story but not the conclusion of the journey. In this very moment, you are on your own journey as well and you get to make choices that will determine where it takes you next.

Whatever you do, know that you are amazing. Not because you are exceptional or extremely talented in one or more areas (which you may very well be) but rather because you showed up. You picked up this book/audio/video/neural download because something, somebody, or some conversation compelled you to do so. So thank you for exploring how to create more human connection today through Talk2MorePeople encounters. You are learning how to help make this world a better place.

Now, with a smile and nothing but loving, positive intentions, I ask of you, please get out there, look up and Talk2MorePeople.

But wait, there's more!

Hey, thanks for reading. I appreciate it, honestly. There are plenty of distractions today that could have kept you from getting this far. My wish is that it was more than worth your while. If you have a story to share about the positive impact that meeting a stranger made on your life, I'd love to hear it. Send me a note at stories@Talk2MorePeople.com.

In closing, I'll use my own advice to offer and then ask for help here. To build self-confidence, learn how to end loneliness and to receive my latest updates, visit Talk2MorePeople.com/community.

Ratings make it easier for readers to discover a book to change their life, and they help the author improve the writing in their next work. Could you please post a rating of this book online? It would be a huge help to me.

Finally, please check out the next section for more connections that will help you reflect on how you can use what you've learned to bring new opportunities, experiences, and people into your life. Happy connecting.

Sincerely,
Tony Esteves

"Your intuition is
always with you,
so why not follow it?"

3 SUCCESS STORIES AND MORE

How could a book about the benefits, tools, and techniques of meeting strangers be complete without the voices of strangers? While I've done my best to illustrate how transformative it is to meet people, that's just my voice and my lived experience. If two heads are better than one, why not have sixteen? Below are a group of contributors who provide further evidence that making face-to-face connections changes lives. Their sweet stories offer a variety of perspectives and possibilities from speaking with new people. Each of the contributors are wonderful humans who have impacted my life, so I'm welcoming you to their conversations.

Renee and I met on Day 305 of the Talk2MorePeople Project in Bragg Creek, Alberta. We developed a strong, loving relationship and have shared many beautiful experiences. Together we have travelled internationally and across Canada by land; house-sat for a full year; spent six weeks exploring van life; and share a home. We have a mutual love of nature, growing and eating food (why have a lawn when you could grow food?), and random adventures. We also both believe that you should work to live and not live to work.

Talking to strangers is so important. Might I even say vital to our life as people? We all desire and need connection! It is part of our nature. Having someone listen, acknowledge what we say, and express their thoughts allows us to reflect, grow, and understand different perspectives. We become more empathetic and realize we are not alone in our thoughts, feelings, or actions. We need to connect to be our fullest selves. It is an incredible feeling to share a moment with a complete stranger, even if nothing is said. It is so important to overcome this fear we create in talking to strangers as the benefits are invaluable.

—Renee Ladouceur

I met Francois a day before presenting at my first-ever creativity conference in 2012, Mindcamp. He attended my juggling/focus session and encouraged me to bring it to the ACRE Creativity Conference in South Africa. Six weeks later, I did so with Francois as my generous host. This was one of the most exciting times of my life, and Francois continues to be a mentor and good friend to me today.

I am an introvert. As someone who likes and enjoys moments of solitude, proactively approaching and meeting people is not a skill that has come naturally to me.

For me to meet and connect to strangers is a painful exercise that I avoid as much as I can. I am very aware that my reluctance to reach out to people I don't know, limits me from having interesting encounters, learnings, and friendships.

Fortunately, this is mitigated by the fact that I love to play sport. Over the years, I have been lucky enough to meet many like-minded and interesting people who were not reluctant to approach me and start up a conversation.

One of the best friendships I have developed came out of a chance encounter that I initiated.

About twenty-five years ago, after a particularly exhausting match in a squash tournament, I sat in the dressing room, ready to undress and have a shower. While I was cooling down, I decided to have a beer. I had a whole case with me, which in South Africa is twenty-four beers. I planned on sharing with my opponent and friends who were playing in the tournament.

As I sat there, a player I did not know walked in and cast an incredulous look at the beer next to me. Seeing that he had just walked off the court as well and feeling generous, I said, "Hey, would you like to have a beer?"

He accepted my invitation, sat down, and we started talking. I found out that he was a fellow squash player playing in a different age group and that he enjoyed the sport as much as I did. One beer became more beers. Between the two of us, we finished the whole case of beer. We failed to notice the squash courts getting quiet and everyone disappearing as afternoon turned into the early evening.

With all the drinks gone, we bid each other farewell, and I certainly did not expect any kind of encounter with him again. But over time, we kept running into each other, and we kept on having drinks after squash tournaments. So we became excellent friends.

Over the years, I have had the good fortune to play with him as a team member for our national club championships. We have shared many trips and sporting memories together.

He also introduced me to his wonderful family, and I have since then spent many enjoyable lunches and dinners at his home and he at mine. His daughters grew up in front of me, and I became a part of their extended family group.

As we got to know each other better, I found out that he was a very successful businessman in his own right. Over the years he has generously shared many lessons and ideas as a mentor, coach, and sounding board. Early on, he shared with me his philosophy on money and debt, which has been an extremely useful lesson. That advice allowed me to turn my financial world upside down and become debt-free in a few years.

I find it funny that, twenty-five years on, one of my best friendships was created by a simple invitation for a drink to a stranger. I very easily could have ignored him at that moment. I am glad I didn't!

—Francois Coetzee, Coach,
NLPWithPurpose.com

Michael and I have shared the stage together as performers and enjoyed many wonderful conversations since then. He has been teaching me about sustainability and tiny homes—since he built his own—and we are good friends to this day.

My experience with Talk2MorePeople started a real transformation in my life. As an introvert, I am comfortable keeping to myself and not talking with strangers if I don't have to. With Tony's program, I was forced out of my comfort zone, and I am so glad for the push. I met amazing people over the thirty days, including one individual who was walking/boating across Canada. I wouldn't have engaged with these people normally, and my life was enriched because of it. Now if I'm standing in line at the grocery store, or waiting for my coffee at Starbucks, I will put down my phone and make an effort to start up a conversation with a stranger. I have Tony to thank for the connections I've made since taking the challenge. If you are tired of the humdrum of day-to-day life and want to feel something real, take his challenge. You never know where it will lead.

—Michael Bartz

Rob came into my life at Mindcamp. He inspires me with his open-mindedness, for how well he communicates, and for living an authentic life.

The light from the midnight campfire danced off the forest canopy. I was on a mission to replenish water supplies for my fellow adult summer campers. I had completed one run with the water cooler, and my internal clock said it was time for another. Well, that and the mostly empty Coleman jug. As I crossed the campfire pit, I noticed her standing alone beside the fire. It was the girl from the bus who said she was unsure why she was coming to camp—hippy-dippy things were apparently not in her wheelhouse. No matter, I was a counsellor this year, and I also knew she ran a charity in the same co-working space that I belonged to back in the city. Not quite a colleague nor acquaintance and yet not entirely a stranger. I felt compelled to check in on her camp experience as the weekend was coming to a close with a raucous DJ campfire party.

"Hey, just thought I'd see how you're doing," I ventured. I don't recall her response. What I do remember is how the seconds turned into minutes and then into what felt like an eternity. We mostly just eye-gazed and swayed with one another by the glowing fire as the ambient techno gave us a beat. We interspersed the gazing with giggles and a rapid exchange on creativity, sacred space, and "being seen." I had never felt so instantly understood by another human in my life. She looked well past my professional veneer of "lawyer" and my animal onesie to the core of my desire to express my true self, to be taken seriously as a creative-thinking professional (even though we were meant to experience no work talk at camp), and to be a sensual human. It feels like a lot happened in that half- to three-quarters hour. Bangarang and Wacky Duck seeing each other for the first time. Noticing our shared soul.

Apparently, we left a little more than swaying and eye-gazing in the memories of our fellow campers who witnessed that connection. I won't kiss and tell! It took a few more text exchanges to arrange our next encounter once we were back in the bustle of our daily lives. Still, things quickly escalated from there and six months out I understood what it meant to have met my soulmate. Not a Disney princess, but someone who would challenge me to live my most authentic self and support me at every step along the way. We have since expanded our soul connection to include a bubbling toddler who challenges, loves, and trusts us with his whole being. We are grateful to be his students, and stewards, for the journey to come.

We attended Camp Reset as imperfect strangers and returned with a timeless commitment to one another. We had reset ourselves.

—Robert Wakulat, Lawyer and Facilitator
DesignWithCourage.com

I met Ginny in 2012 at my first Mindcamp in an Image Streaming session facilitated by the amazing Dr. Win Wenger. We quickly became friends and then colleagues. Ginny continues to be a creative role model for me on how to live a healthy life. As an expert holistic coach and facilitator, she is the reason I began to eat properly in my mid-forties—literally extending my life (potential). When I hit one hundred, I'll have Ginny to thank.

I was inside a community centre in Toronto with my two boys and my stepson, trying to keep them entertained and out of trouble. At the time, my stepdaughter played soccer in the gym. We were eating snacks while playing a card game. I consider myself quite shy and introverted. The fact that I speak Spanish to my kids helps keep our conversations private in most public spaces. In my professional role, as a creativity and change leadership consultant, I can get up and speak to hundreds of people in English, no problem. But if you ask me to approach a stranger, I really need to build up the courage. I have no idea why, but just the thought of speaking to a stranger makes me break into a sweat. It feels like my heart stops and I hold my breath.

The chatter in my head goes something like this: let them be, they don't want to be interrupted or bothered by someone they've never met, your accent will throw them off, and they won't even know what you said, and then you will have to repeat yourself and make a fool of yourself, everyone in the room will turn around and notice you, do not draw attention to yourself, why bother, we are perfectly fine, there's no need to meet anyone new. Despite the inner fear-mongering chatter, I am well aware of the importance of stepping out of your comfort zone to learn new things, have new experiences. In this case, I knew the boys were starting to get a little bored and loud. It was too cold to go outside. And I was always looking for ways of encouraging my kids to be curious and open to learning something new. I had to be a good role model for them.

There was a dad and a son sitting next to us. I noticed the boy eyeing us discreetly. Maybe he wanted to join in and play with us. Perhaps he was wondering what language we were speaking. I had been silently admiring how patient he and his dad appeared to be up until then, both engrossed in separate *National Geographic* magazines. Since it's always easier to speak to a child than to an adult, I started off by asking the kid how old he was, what grade he was in, what school he went to, and whether he wanted to play with us. It turned out he was ten, the same age as my older son and stepson. Great! We already had something in common.

The dad, who I now know as Vikas, quickly joined into the conversation and asked my kids a few questions. A level of trust was instantly formed among all six of us. He immediately jumped into asking the kids fascinating questions about astronomy and the laws of physics. He managed to capture all the kids' curiosity in just a few seconds. He was also quick to compliment them for their intelligence and insightfulness—this, of course, deepened their trust in him. We all dropped the game and engaged in a fascinating inquiry into the laws of physics, black holes, and meteorites. I admired Vikas's approach to asking questions. I noticed that he never gave the kids his knowledge or opinion. Instead, he answered every one of their questions with a new question that led them to come up with their own answers. I grew to appreciate more and more his way of teaching the kids how to think and learn by encouraging their curiosity, rather than force-feeding them knowledge and information.

I then came to learn that Vikas and his kids spent most of their free time building robots and engaging in creative projects. Instead of buying a TV for their living room, they purchased a 3D printer. What started off as a polite conversation turned into a long-lasting friendship. We exchanged emails and started getting together for family dinners and creative events. The kids love getting together to climb trees just as much as sitting with the latest robot to explore its parts and mechanics.

—Ginny Santos, MSc Creativity and Innovation
CEO at NeOle Inc.
Neole.ca

Rob and his twin brother, Dave, came into my life when my travels began in Whistler, British Columbia, back in 1998. Close friends ever since, we have been housemates in London, England; Toronto, Ontario; and Calgary, Alberta; and have had many random, hilarious adventures. Rob is one of the hardest-working, most genuine people I know. He more than anyone I've ever met lives life on his own terms and embraces random life experiences. We plan to retire together.

Some people are lucky enough to meet people they know will become instant lifelong friends. I am lucky because I have more than most. One of the first lifelong friends I met when I was fifteen. I met Mark through a friend-of-a-friend scenario because of a random decision to hang with a group of teens I didn't always hang out with. He worked hard through the week, and relaxed and partied on the weekends. Not someone you would think would be keen on ensuring we all stayed in school. But he believed an education to be part of a successful life.

He ended up teaching me how to drive a manual transmission car, and other social and life skills, but mainly to just have respect for myself and others. Through meeting him, I've had the pleasure of seeing him get married and raise a great family. To this day, thirty years later, I can still just call up and continue from where we left off. The only difference is, I now also have his wife and son in the lifelong friend group. I could go on about how I met so many lifelong friends by chance, luck, a random decision, or through a job; however, there are great examples in this book. Just remember sometimes random is a good life choice.

—Rob Gregory, Random Life Expert

Andrea is my twin sister. We were womb-mates before we were born and have been very close friends and each other's source of inspiration and support ever since. She is an incredibly intelligent, powerful and soulful woman who I am proud to call "Twin."

One of my favourite out-of-the-blue connections with a stranger was with a woman I met on a plane. I believe it started by me asking her where she was off to and that was all we needed to start our chat. We were flying from Toronto to Calgary and it was 2012. I was flying back to Fort McMurray for my admin job in the oil sands via Calgary after visiting my family in Ontario. She—Soria, I believe her name was—was flying to Vancouver Island to visit a cherished girlfriend and meet a man she'd been corresponding with for a while online. She was an HR p, so I think that made our connection easy.

We ended up eating lunch together as we continued our conversations. We laughed a bit and just felt like we'd known each other a long time, though it had literally orofessional, very open, and kind. We hit it off chatting about life, our life paths. We were close in age (mid-thirties) and both born and raised and university-educated in Canada, people-lovers, and positive and kindness-motivatednly been minutes. I think that we felt that way because we both entered with open minds about the other and were secure in ourselves. We weren't looking to judge each other or seek validation or get anything out of each other but were just genuinely curious about each other's experiences. We talked about careers, health, happiness and relationships. The conversation flowed so easily. It was such a lovely experience.

I remember at that time I was sad I was flying back to a job/workplace I was quite unhappy in, but our connection helped me recharge and go back up with more hope in my spiritual tank. Although usually stubbornly positive, I absolutely appreciated and needed the positivity infusion that Soria gave me that day. That insight (that I need connection with others), however, was something I didn't consciously realize until a few years later. Anyhow, in the line of happiness and health, she recommended a website I might enjoy called DailyGood.org and it became one of my favourite sites. It's a secular website celebrating the beauty of humanity and life. The Good News website. It's amazing and I share it with anyone I can.

Also, she had to leave the lunch a bit early to catch her flight. And when I went to pay my portion, I found out she had covered it for me. The kindness of strangers is so lovely, isn't it? We see what we look for, I believe, and looking for the best in others, kindness, has always served me well.

—Andrea Esteves
Communications Consultant

Tru and I met on Day 142 of the Talk2MorePeople Project through a mutual friend in Toronto, Garth Sam. What an introduction that turned out to be! We have celebrated and supported each other in more ways than I can count. A very talented young-at-heart-musician in his mid-sixties, with the vitality of someone in their mid-thirties, Tru brought music back into my life, leads a heart-centred community, and has shared a great deal of wisdom with me. I have greatly enjoyed sharing the writing process with him, listening to his beautiful original music, and dwelling in the deep conversations that we so readily enjoy.

In the spring of 2016, I was irresistibly called and drawn to release myself of most of my possessions, my Toronto residence, and a woman with whom I had been having a deeply loving relationship for over two years (a blessing that also became catalytic in my deciding to depart on my journey).

It was becoming clear to me that I needed to connect with the world on a more personal level, and I needed to more deeply understand where I was and what I thought I knew about life and myself, by going beyond my familiar patterns of association and comfort.

I was stepping out on faith with no timetable and no predictable agenda, other than complete receptivity to how I could serve what I was "feeling" to be my evolving purpose. Trusting, trusting, trusting, every step of the way. It was a leap into the unknown of my capacity to remain open to meeting the world with an unconditional and loving heart.

Every encounter with strangers as I travelled across Canada became an opportunity to observe with no agenda, to appreciate things from a fresh perspective and an open mind by looking through the windows of other people's experience. It also became increasingly clear as to why I was meeting one or more people at any particular time. We almost always had something to share that would become mutually edifying, even if it was just a simple moment of acknowledgement in the silent realms of each other's speechless presence.

Every encounter became a piece in the puzzle of my own story.

A reflection of where I was in myself.

It measured my capacity to let go, to laugh, to care or not to, and to take things in on a deeper level, from discovering a more profound understanding that things are often perfect just as they are.

Every new encounter spoke to how universally connected we all are.

Encountering strangers revealed an amazing thing. We are not static beings to be here only for ourselves. We are evolving beings and intimately connected to each other's growth.

All my encounters with strangers on the road taught me that the guiding principles of life always have a way of allowing us to work things out, in our own way, when we do it with a deep respect for all life.

Coincidence became synchronicity in my willingness to connect with others. I was finding more and more people who were kindred souls and, in a very timely way, entering my life exactly when it was most needed and appreciated.

One such example was when I arrived at a campground in Thunder Bay two months into my journey. I heard a clunk at the back end of my Jeep and knew something had just broken. I happened to be speaking with a gentleman on the phone whom I had stayed with on the reserve in Sault St. Marie. He hooked me up with another person, who called me and said there was a man at the very campground where I was who was a mechanic. I went in search and found him, and after chatting for a while, I asked if he could help me out. He turned to me and to my surprise said, "As you can see, I am restoring this 1956 Ford and am very busy, but as you were talking, an angel came into my presence and told me I have to help you out, so I will."

As he was checking under my Jeep, he turned to me with wide eyes and said, "You are lucky to be alive!" "What do you mean?" I asked.

"You have a huge hole rusted out at your tail pipe. You've been breathing in carbon dioxide!"

"That explains why I was getting so sleepy while I was driving," I reflected back. In essence this stranger saved my life, and he didn't charge me a cent, except for the parts. As I write this, many tears of gratitude fall.

Not long after I arrived in Calgary, I met Tony Esteves through a mutual friend's long-distance introduction. Tony was nearing halfway with his Talk2MorePeople Project when we met in person. Since our first meeting, a beautiful friendship has emerged and we have worked together on a number of community events with great success, the most recent of which was my labour of love event called HeartFest, a festival for and from the Heart, where Tony did a Talk2MorePeople workshop and an improv performance beyond anything he has done before.

Tony brings such heart and integrity into everything he does. He was one stranger who I now get to call a dear friend and brother. The privilege and opportunity to meet him has enriched my life beyond measure.

So, to put my experiences in meeting strangers into a nutshell: to get to the "nut" (meeting strangers and great connections), you have to break the shell that has held you back from taking the risk.

It's like swimming. Just jump in; before you know it, you'll learn how to relax into yourself while appreciating the people you're meeting as you swim along.

—Tru Guy Stefanowich Starhorse
Music Messenger and Troubadour of Light and Love

Trent and I met at the Facilitation Exchange. I have learned so much from him, and both of us have celebrated the new people who have come into our lives through the mixing of friend and colleague groups. Trent is an expert international facilitator and motorbike enthusiast.

My story about meeting a stranger that brought good things into my life is actually a story about how I met Tony himself.

And as far as strangers go, Tony is stranger than most! ;-) But in a (very) good way.

We met initially over a mini Ping-Pong table, which is a staple in Tony's repertoire. We happened to both attend a meeting of the Facilitation Exchange, a meet-up group for professional facilitators. The gist of the meetings is for attendees to share a technique or lead a discussion. This time it was Tony's turn. After a preamble where he began to whet our appetites for what was to come, Tony unleashed us on a set of miniature Ping-Pong tables. What followed was a unique facilitated journey where he artfully combined various Ping-Pong–centred activities with guided reflections that provided great insights into ourselves and how we think and do.

I was impressed. We agreed to reconnect.

Yeah, I know. People do this all the time and never follow up. And that's a shame.

But we did make it happen. And it has grown into a wonderful friendship with multiple professional collaborations.

So what's the lesson? (Give me a moment to put on my facilitator hat.) The next time you connect and then part ways with a vague commitment to get together sometime, don't just say it. Actually do it! There's a good chance that it will open the door to a whole new world of experiences.

—Trent Schumann, BSc, Coach for High Achievers
Team/Leadership development: experienca.com
Passion Project: wanduro.com
Coaching: joydividend.com

I reluctantly went out one evening while living in Toronto, and Ian and I were introduced by my housemate Bob. We hit it off like old friends that first night of fun and, after a sushi meeting, decided to become housemates. This began an international friendship that continues today.

Having spent most of the past twenty-four years travelling or being involved in travel to some capacity, I've met countless new friends who have all caused a ripple in my ever-expanding ocean of an existence, some of which have led to tidal waves of change and personal growth. With almost too many to count, the best to probably highlight would be one of the first people I met in my early travels who really pushed my own comfort zones and outlook on the world.

I had just celebrated my twentieth birthday in the foothills of the Himalayas in northern India when I met Matthias. Just a few years older, he already had the presence of a wise, old shaman, much like the sadhus I had seen meditating on the village streets where I was staying. We had found ourselves in McLeod Ganj, a village where the Dalai Lama and many other Tibetans had taken refuge forty years prior. As cliché as it may be, it was the perfect setting for the first real step of learning on my own journey, much of which would be filled with hardship, challenges, and other things inherent to life on this planet.

We ended up travelling across the northern half of India together on a journey that would last a little more than a month. When we met, he had already travelled by land all the way from Munich, through pretty challenging regions. Our conversations were likely just filled with small talk—where to eat next, what hotel to stay in, and so forth—but every now and then, something profound would be discussed.

I remember one situation, which will probably turn your heads in disgust, but please bear with me. We had found ourselves in the Golden Temple—a Sikh temple on the border of Pakistan. It was open to all visitors, and you could even sleep inside the temple. Both food and accommodation were free, if you didn't mind eating off plates with your hand (note: in India, you eat with your right hand) and sleeping on thin mats on the ground. There are no real expectations of a return, though if you want to maintain your own good karma, you should leave a relatively decent donation to the temple upon leaving (we paid more than we may have for the same meals and a nicer hotel room when we left, simply out of respect to the temple and the experience it provided us).

The situation arose when I had to use the bathroom. Upon entering, I noticed the squat toilets you become all too familiar with travelling through certain parts of the world. That wasn't the issue, however. It was the small bucket and tap of water—or more so, the lack of toilet paper. With the situation not being overly urgent, I returned to the room to ask for some toilet paper from Matthias. He obliged, and I went about my business, but it was upon my return that we had our chat. "I understand your hesitation, but as a society it's really saddening, isn't it?" he began. "For millions of years, as with all life on this planet, we have had natural functions. At what point in time did we become so disconnected with ourselves that we can't even touch ourselves to be hygienic?" I argued that the mere act itself was unhygienic, though he quickly snapped back that the water was there for cleaning—and you're intended to soap up your left hand after (and for the added hygiene precautionary measures, that's why you eat, and greet people, with your right). I saw his point.

I'm not saying I have now lived by his words, but it was his perspective that changed me. I was so quick to shun and judge another culture for doing something that is, by all definitions of the term, natural. It was an important stepping stone in being able to open up to others' differences—without necessarily agreeing with them or participating, I could at least begin to appreciate them on a deeper level. That really did change my life, and is only one example of many conversations we shared in that month travelling together. A stranger when we met, though a cornerstone in my own development by the end! I'm happy we randomly connected and decided to take that adventure together, as I don't know how I would be able to do what I do now otherwise, or if I would have connected with the people I have met since in the same way.

—Ian Ord, Founder and Travel Guru, Where Sidewalks End
Wheresidewalksend.com

Tracey and Dave are fantastic people! We have had more laughs together than I have with anyone I've met on the Talk2MorePeople Project (with the exception of my partner). Tracey is our mindfulness guru who shares mindfulness techniques in the Appendix.

We went to a TGIF evening hosted by our good friend Trent. While we were there, we ran into an energetic, intriguing person who introduced himself as Tony, which spelled backwards is Y-NOT?! We had a very engaging conversation with him, and he mentioned that he was looking for people to join his improv jam. We had been talking about improv a few weeks prior, so decided that it was meant to be for us to join Tony's jam.

Little did we know that a few months later. Tony would be part of our inner circle of friends. Since meeting Tony, we have enjoyed many fun improv jams, interesting dinner parties. and colourful social gatherings. Tony is a great improv coach. The various improv exercises we have done with him have helped us to be more spontaneous and confident in public speaking situations, office meetings. and with meeting new people. More importantly, he has brought a lot of fun and laughter into our lives.

Tony's Talk2MorePeople Project is more important than ever, as people pay more attention to their phones than to the person sitting beside them. He has inspired us to put in a sincere effort to connect with strangers. As a result, we have had many amazing conversations, learned new things along the way, and have felt closer to the people around us. Our experience has been that every connection with another person brings out more compassion, empathy, and understanding within ourselves.

Connecting with fellow human beings is one of the foundations of true happiness.

We are grateful for being part of Tony's life and to be Day 227 of his Talk2MorePeople Project. Our lives have been enriched as a result of Tony connecting with us. Everybody needs a Tony in their life, so get off your phone and talk to a stranger, and be open to expanding your possibilities!

—Tracey Delfs and Dave Van Den Assem
BalanceQuest.com

Eily and I met on stage while performing at Freezer Burn—Alberta's regional Burning Man Festival—in 2017. Eily brings stunning harp music and energy healing to the people she works with and leads an international community of artistic, human connection.

I live life believing friends are everywhere. And one wintery Calgary morning, I met up with four new friends on the train heading west. After finishing an early morning cleaning job, I longingly awaited sitting down and eating my breakfast on the warm train. As soon as I boarded, I noticed a woman with a fast-food breakfast sandwich to my left. Encouraged, I said, "Oh, someone else who hasn't eaten breakfast. Do you mind if I sit next to you? Let's eat together!"

She smiled and said, "Sure! I had to grab this as it was a busy morning. I understand how it is."

"It looks delicious," I replied.

After taking off my warm gloves, I reached into my backpack to open my unusual breakfast of quinoa, almond milk, and tahini. My new friend leaned over. "That's an interesting breakfast," she said.

"Yeah. It's one of my favourites," I said.

As the seats of the train were facing lengthwise, it was easy to notice two people opposite (and one woman who was standing) being pulled into the conversation with friendly glances and smiles as my new friend and I continued to talk about our breakfast and the daily commute.

"What did you have for breakfast?" I asked the man sitting opposite me, noticing a smile above his newspaper.

"Just cereal," he said. "The same as I have every day. Not very interesting."

"What about you?" I asked the woman who was standing. Maybe because English seemed to be her second language, she smiled at me and looked back at the changing scenery.

One man wearing overalls, steel-toed boots, and a construction hat called from nearly halfway down the train car, "I didn't even have time for breakfast!"

"Oh no!" I said, "You better eat something before you head off to the site."

"Yeah, I know," he said, as the train came to a stop and he headed off with a big bag of tools. A friendly "Have a great day!" followed behind him and his friend as they left.

The man sitting opposite me continued to talk about his daily commute until he headed off at the next stop with a warm "You have a wonderful rest of your trip!" I couldn't help but take notice of his shift in mood. Was that really the same guy who only minutes before was grimly reading the morning newspaper?

All four friends were now on their way to work. And there I was, still eating the last of my breakfast as the train neared my stop. I am so glad I remembered that new friends are only a smile and a question away. Next time I'll bring extra breakfast to share.

—Eily Aurora, Social Innovator and Harp Faery
EilyAurora.com
Instagram.com/theharpfaery

Patrick has become a great and supportive friend of mine. We have performed many times together with Le Cirque de la Nuit and shared communities with one another. It's not every day that you meet a new friend while in makeup for a photoshoot. Patrick is a talented photographer, educator, and one of the kindest, most generous people I know.

On June 15, 2014, I attended Calgary Circus School's year-end show, where circus students perform and get a chance to demonstrate the skills they have been learning. It was there that I met Alix, a photographer and a member of Le Cirque de la Nuit. We got talking and she invited me for a photoshoot. Unfortunately, our contact information exchange did not work out and we did not end up being able to get in touch with each other. But then, in September, while walking around downtown in the East Village, I ran into Alix again! This time we exchanged numbers and on March 14, 2015, I visited her studio for a photoshoot. It was at this photoshoot that I would meet Tony Esteves. He and I have since become close friends. As a result of this photoshoot, I have gotten involved and performed with the circus. This has been a great experience for me that started by randomly meeting a new person.

—Patrick Chan, Educator

Ian and I met through a mutual friend and bouldering—an activity that I had wanted to try for years but didn't think I had the time to do. He introduced me to the world of creativity where countless other new connections and friendships and professional growth arose.

Yesterday I was out for a ride to Rockaway Beach. I was twenty minutes into my ride, near Prospect Park, and saw a posse—a gang, if you will—of fellow two-wheeled *rolleurs.* I don't know where I saw it and yet somehow knew they were also riding to the beach. I stopped about 200 feet after them and thought, *It would be good to meet some new peeps. Do I really want to talk to new people today?* All the usual chatter that keeps me stuck in my own head. I turned around and, with my own unique blend of humour and wit, asked (1) if they were a posse, (2) if they were going to the beach, (3) how did I know this, and (4) if I could join them. Turns out they were, and I went along with them! So, thanks to you, Tony, for influencing my decision to go back and talk to them. Because of you, I have a glorious sunburn today.

—Ian Rosenfeldt, Designer, Facilitator, Human

Will is another man who makes puns. He is a fun person with a great sense of humour, an eye for adventure and is also an accomplished professional. We lived in nearby towns in inaka (rural) Japan for two years as English teachers on the JET Programme. He, along with several other people I met from that work experience remain some of the best friends in my life today. We have enjoyed many outdoor adventures together on three continents.

I arrived in Australia back in 2016 to take up a role with a global management consulting firm, with very few friends or even acquaintances locally and my family back in the UK who would be joining me in a couple of months. I took up beach volleyball, thinking it a quintessentially Aussie thing to do, and because I know I'm rubbish at cricket. Saturday mornings were spent in the glorious sunshine on the scorching sand with an eclectic mix of volleyballers, though very few actual Australians. Standing in the queue to practise our drills of set-ups, spikes, and smashes, I would invariably ask the person I was partnered with how long they'd been in Coogee (the beachy suburb of Sydney), Sydney, or just Australia, and then what they "did" that brought them to Australia. Usually my guess at placing the accent was wrong, but it'd start the conversation and some enduring friendships started there, four years ago.

One practice session I was paired with a tall Indian chap who introduced himself as Muneesh (turns out he'd been in Australia for over twenty years). We exchanged where we're from and what we did for a living, our conversation rudely interrupted by actually having to play volleyball. As we took to the court, he started telling me about the organization he'd started called Humanity in Business. Now, I like to think I've always had a moral, values-based approach to my career and am keen to "help" the community and society and make a positive impact (though I lack the courage or time to permanently volunteer or retrain as a nurse). Muneesh explained his vision and aspirations with Humanity in Business to bring the skills and experience of commercial organization to benefit not-for-profit organizations and charities, and in so doing enhance their own leadership, professional skills, and sense of purpose. Needless to say, this really chimed with my ambitions to find more purpose in my corporate career and piqued my interest. Muneesh was equally interested in my background with the British Army and now in management consulting as being an avenue to access business expertise to help solve some of the operating challenges faced by local charities and not-for-profits. We exchanged phone numbers and met up for coffee a few weeks later to deepen the conversation.

A few months later, he sent me an invitation to an event he was holding to support local charities' progress in some of their challenges. I managed to rally a dozen management consultants and, along with other participating firms, we all enjoyed a constructive day meeting and hopefully helping those who are working on the front line to improve our local Sydney communities, from designing a new fundraising strategy for a young person's mental health charity to refreshing the marketing campaign of a local domestic abuse support organization. I certainly found it to be a challenging, inspiring, and rewarding day. Roll forward eighteen months and I'm with a new firm working in learning and development and have introduced Muneesh to a colleague who is developing a program to build leadership skills. With Humanity in Business, we are now exploring developing a program to pair professionals in our firm with local not-for-profits to enhance their leadership and commercial skills and support those organizations. We are looking forward to the next chapter, and when we meet up for coffee, always the first question is whether we are still playing volleyball.

—Will Henry, People Developer

GRATITUDE

Many people have helped me connect these words through shared experiences, encouragement, love, and support. If you get a chance to connect with any of these souls, you will be pleased that you did.

First and foremost, I must acknowledge my dear partner, Renee Ladouceur, for supporting me in all aspects of my life, and with the creation of this book, and for all of the laughter that we have shared. She created warm and loving environments for me to get these words together, gave me space when I needed to focus on the writing, and encouraged me when I had doubts about the need to complete this work. While I'm sure those doubts are common to many authors, they felt unique to me and yet manageable, thanks to Renee.

I want to acknowledge both of my parents, Mary-Barbara and Tony Esteves. When I was a child, they allowed me to frolic in the forest until dark and to get my hands dirty. They taught me how to play, which has become such an important part of who I am as an adult today. I think about and fondly remember my dear old dad often. He taught me how to work hard physically, as well as how to forgive others easily. With his openness, and his bold and occasionally offensive authenticity, he showed me how amazing and beautiful people are.

I offer the sincerest thanks to my twin, Andrea Esteves, for being my best friend since we were womb-mates. She is the reason that I moved to Calgary, which brought me close to the breathtaking Rocky Mountains that offer me so much inspiration and revitalization. She introduced me to the transformational Hoffman Process, which helped me past a writing hurdle and into a place of authentic self-love. Finally, Andrea is always inspiring and challenging me to be the best person that I can be.

Thank you to these contributors who took the time to offer a segment in the Success Stories section: Renee Ladouceur, Francois Coetzee, Michael Bartz, Robert Wakulat, Ginny Santos, Rob Gregory, Andrea Esteves, Tru Guy Stefanowich Starhorse, Trent Schumann, Ian Ord, Tracey Delfts (who also contributed the Appendix on mindfulness), Dave Van Den Assem, Eily Aurora, Patrick Chan, Will Henry, and Ian Rosenfeldt for the conversation that led me to creativity. I must also thank the entire Mindcamp creativity community for the many ideas and people who I've met that have enriched my heart, my mind, and my life.

For other anecdotes throughout the book, reflections, and support, thanks go to Jon Stromberg (for teaching me to juggle); Julian from Germany (who took me across Canada by bicycle); Josh Buyze and Chris Veitch (my housemates during the Project); Marnie Parsons; Laura Downing; Jude Vanderweg; Dolphin Kasper; David Croney; Keith Bendall; Ryan Jeans (Mr. miniPong); Karen Jacobs; Doug Wong; Mike Wilkes (for helping me get back into improv); Chris Snoyer; Ashley Victoria (for the conversation that led me to the circus); Ivan Hawkes; Allen Porayko; Stephen from England; Jesse Keefer; Jan Keck; Mollie Kaye and fellow performers Bitch Sassidy and Braden Lyster (aka Troo Knot).

I'd like to send out hugs and high-fives to Tammara Francis, Pete Nazarewycz, and Brogan Graham from the November Project for all of the connections they have created through fitness. Thanks to Keoma and Bill Deuce (in whose home much of the writing took place while house-sitting); Patricia Morgan (for holding me accountable); and Kate McKenzie (for suggesting I create a card for the 30-Day Challenge). Thank you, Jennifer Powter, for suggesting that I read *The War of Art*. Thanks to Kurt Archer for years of technical and design support.

I'm also grateful for everyone who I've met through my work with Le Cirque de la Nuit. This includes the many talented circus performers, skillful technical crew and build team, costume designers, choreographers, photographers and videographers, hair and makeup artists, and volunteers. In particular, I want to acknowledge the original troupe who were at my audition and welcomed me on board: Jai Benteau, Kelley Matley, Chad Shier, Alix Broadway, Tasheena Dunn, Bernice Welacky, Shannon Reinhold, Julie Mercier, Jessica Bedford, Devin Giles, and Sarah Benteau. The experience of performing in events with so many moving pieces, surrounded by this much creative talent, has been a true honour.

Thanks to Geordie Keith (whom I met on T2MP Day 252), Francois Coetzee and Karin Roest for being excellent coaches for me over the years. Brian Keiller provided much-needed last-minute feedback of the fourth draft that was a huge help. Thanks to Sylvie Vidal for the wonderful, unexpected adventure in France. Thank you to Haesun Moon, from the Canadian Centre for Brief Coaching, for teaching me how to be a more effective coach, and how to have more impactful conversations. This influenced the final writing in this book.

The book you are reading now would not have been possible without my editor, Erin Parker. She worked with me to craft my ideas into a useful format and was an absolute pleasure to work with. A dear friend, editor, and author, Ruth Zuchter, has also provided editorial advice and support over the years for which I am truly grateful. She guided me long before this book was anywhere near to becoming a book. I also have gratitude for Carra Simpson for helping me get this book as professionally produced as possible through her project management. Palmo Carpino patiently gave me countless cover design ideas and revisions and made the inside and outside of the book look beautiful enough for people to pick it up. Thanks to Ruth Wilson for the excellent job of proofreading.

Obrigado to Daniel Nobre who shot the portrait on the back cover. And thanks to Jenny Sager for creating the costume in that portrait. Patrick Chan kindly captured the Mirror Man photo and Olga Sem created the mirror suit. The Mr. Moonstache photo is courtesy of Le Cirque de la Nuit. The reflections photos in nature are the author's. You saw Berg Glacier on Mt. Robson in British Columbia, as well as Lake Louise, Alberta and Upper Kananaskis, Lake, Alberta on the back cover.

I would like to acknowledge the thousands of strangers I have met before, during, and since the Talk2MorePeople Project. You have helped shape, improve, and influence my life in so many ways, and this continues to help me grow towards my potential. In doing so, you have enabled me to support others in finding and expressing their voice and potential as well. How generous it was of you to take some time out of your busy day to engage with me in a random conversation. Whenever and wherever we met, you helped me write this book, which is the most significant way that I can make a positive contribution to the world today. What an incredible gift you unknowingly gave me through our chance encounter. Thank you.

And I offer my thanks to you, the reader, for taking the time to explore this book and to play with the concepts. An idea only matters if it is put into action. By fully reading through this material, you've got the greatest opportunity to put the learning into action and create a ripple effect of positivity.

Finally, I'd like to acknowledge the land where most of this book was written, which was Calgary, Alberta, Canada. There were Indigenous people here thousands of years before we were and I believe that it's important to mention that. If you are not already familiar, you can research the history of the land that you are living on now and find out how to appropriately acknowledge the land. It is important to do this. Take time to learn about Indigenous issues in your region as there are many injustices that need to be resolved today.

Below is a land acknowledgement for the Calgary region from the Calgary Foundation:

In the spirit of respect, reciprocity, and truth, we honour and acknowledge Moh'kinsstis and the traditional Treaty 7 territory and oral practices of the Blackfoot confederacy: Siksika, Kainai, Piikani, as well as the Îyâxe Nakoda and Tsuut'ina nations. We acknowledge that this territory is home to the Métis Nation of Alberta, Region 3, within the historical Northwest Métis homeland. Finally, we acknowledge all Nations, Indigenous and non, who live, work, and play, as well as help steward this land, honour, and celebrate this territory.

This sacred gathering place provides us with an opportunity to engage in and demonstrate leadership on reconciliation. Thank you for your enthusiasm and commitment to join our team on the lands of Treaty 7 territory.

Yours in connection,
Tony Esteves

APPENDIX: MINDFULNESS MATTERS, by Tracey Delfs _____

People who practise mindfulness tend to be happier, healthier, and more present than those who don't.

My passion for the last couple of decades has been to bring mindfulness and meditation to corporations, Olympians, and the general public. Therefore, I was excited when Tony asked me to share mindfulness exercises with you. If you integrate these exercises into your life, it will increase your ability to be more present in your Talk2MorePeople encounters and with the people in your life. The greatest gift that we can give anyone is our "presence" with a "c," not with a "t."

My mindfulness journey began in the '90s when I read a book called *Peace Is Every Step* by world-renowned Zen Master Thich Nhat Hanh. He is known as "The Father of Mindfulness." After I read his book, I decided that I had found my teacher and hopped on a plane to visit Plum Village, his mindfulness centre in France. It's been an honour to study regularly with Thay (Vietnamese for "teacher") for over two decades and to share his mindfulness teachings with thousands of people around the world via my virtual one-on-one mindfulness coaching, online programs, and retreats. Now I get the opportunity to share his teachings with you.

Let's begin our mindfulness journey by looking at what mindfulness is. In its simplest terms, mindfulness is being aware of what's happening in this moment. Instead of being present, the mind usually focuses on plans and anxieties of the future or would-have, could-have, should-have regrets from the past. When you practise mindfulness, you learn how to bring your mind back to your body and be fully present in this moment, the most crucial moment of your life.

If our mind is caught up in worries, regrets, or our to-do lists, it robs us of our ability to enjoy the present moment. We may be so caught up in our thoughts that we miss seeing the beautiful sunrise, enjoying the taste of our food, hearing the birds chirping, or looking into the eyes of the people we love. Life is precious; each day we are given 1,440 minutes, and at the end of the day, those moments disappear. Therefore, we must learn to live more in the here and now, so we can enjoy as many of those moments as possible. Life is, after all, the sum of these small moments.

I mentioned before that mindfulness is about creating more awareness in your life—more awareness of your thoughts, emotions, body sensations, and what's happening with the people and the world around you. To increase your level of awareness, you can practise mindfulness formally or informally.

Formal mindfulness practice is when you intentionally set aside time in your day to sit, focus on your breath, relax your body, and observe your thoughts. Formal mindfulness practices include breath awareness, body scans, mindful yoga, and meditation. Later, I will be teaching you how to do a seated body scan and share tips for creating a home meditation practice.

Informal mindfulness meditation is when you practise mindfulness without carving out a particular time for it. Earlier in the book, Tony shared with you how he realized that he was practising informal mindfulness in his day while "in the zone" doing the activities that he loves to do, such as juggling, hiking, and gardening. If you're looking for a quick and easy way to add a little mindfulness to your day, then you may be interested in trying out the following mindfulness exercises.

Informal Mindfulness Practices

There's a great story that someone had asked a Zen Master "What do you and your monks do?" He replied, "We sit, we walk, and we eat." The questioner continued, "But, sir, everyone sits, walks, and eats," and the Zen Master told him, "The difference is that when we sit, we know we are sitting; when we walk, we know we are walking; and when we eat, we know we are eating."[63] Our focus is to practise mindfulness in each moment—to know what is going on within and all around. I find this story sums up the essence of what the informal mindfulness practices are all about.

If you want to train your mind to be more present to help improve your focus, productivity, and communication with others, then you may consider trying to integrate a few of the following informal mindfulness practices into your day.

Mindful Tea Drinking

Find a quiet and comfortable place to sit with your tea. Put away your phone, computer, or any other distractions. When you pick up your tea, you may like to take a deep breath to bring your mind back to your body and become completely present in the here and the now. Let go of all your worries and anxieties and give yourself this gift of time to "just be" and enjoy drinking your tea.

Feel the warmth and smoothness of the cup in your hands. Take your first sip as you feel the warmth of the tea in your mouth, then feel it move down your throat and into your stomach.

Savour your tea as you sip it, noticing the aroma and taste of the drink. Take your time and notice as you get close to being done your tea if it makes you feel energized or calm.

Many years ago, I heard and immediately loved the saying "The way we do something is the way we do everything," which means if you can learn to be fully present with your cup of tea, then you can learn how to be fully present with whomever you're communicating with. Who knew that tea drinking was training for your Talk2MorePeople connections?

Mindful Dishwashing

Do you dread doing tasks around your home such as cleaning, washing clothes, or doing the dishes? We need to realize that these chores and others make up a big part of our life, so we might as well learn to be fully present and start enjoying them. It reminds me of something the Buddha is thought to have said about chores: "Before enlightenment, chop wood, carry water. After enlightenment, chop wood, carry water."

Florida State University did a research study with fifty-one college students on mindful dishwashing.[64] More than half of them were given a passage by Thich Nhat Hanh: "While washing the dishes, one should only be washing the dishes, which means one should be completely aware of the fact that one is washing dishes." This passage inspired them to bring mindfulness into washing the dishes by sensing the water temperature on their hands, smelling the soap, and washing each dish mindfully instead of rushing to get them done.

The control group studied a message that focused on getting things done. The results showed that those who read Thich Nhat Hanh's passage and, as a result, washed their dishes mindfully reported a 25 percent increase in mental inspiration and a 27 percent decrease in nervousness.

Therefore, it's time to do a perspective shift around doing your dishes. Instead of being stressed out by that pile of dishes, it can help with stress reduction. I encourage you to write out Thich Nhat Hanh's quote on a sticky note, place it by your sink, and start mindful dishwashing today!

I like to think about dishwashing as a bubble bath for my hands. I use a dish soap that has a scent that I love and fill the sink with hot water and lots of bubbles! Sometimes I even light a candle by the sink and put on my favourite tunes.

Whether you're washing dishes, shovelling snow, or folding laundry, try to slow down, become more aware of your senses, find joy in whatever you're doing, and make each task an active meditation. This is much more enjoyable than rushing through it to get on to the next thing. Life is precious; don't forget to show up for every moment of it.

As Thich Nhat Hanh says, "Don't hurry, enjoy the present moment."[65]

Mindful Outdoor Walking

Often when we're walking, we hurry. Our mind is on where we need to get to instead of enjoying the journey along the way. Practising mindful walking helps to take us out of a kind of "sleepwalking" state and wakes us up to be more aware of what we are feeling within our body and of what is happening in the world around us.

To practise mindful walking, start by becoming aware of your feet touching the ground and walk slower and lighter than you usually would. Thich Nhat Hanh says, "Imagine that you're kissing the ground with your feet."[66] Feel a sense of gratitude for Mother Earth and the magic of the world around you. Walk with an attitude of peace and joy versus one of stress and worry.

Focus on your breath along with your steps. As you breathe in the oxygen from the trees around you, feel the connection to them. Practising mindfulness helps us feel more connected to the world around us. Walk in silence while you listen to birds, the sound of the river, and the children laughing in the distance. Feel the warmth of the sun or slight breeze on your face. Notice the clouds passing by and the light shining on buildings, and see the shadows on the ground.

When your mind wanders off into the future or the past, just let the thoughts go and bring your awareness back to the sensations of your next step and breathe. An essential part of any mindfulness practice is to find joy in it. Enjoy your walking!

Mindful Toothbrushing

We start and end our day with brushing our teeth. Therefore, if we brush our teeth mindfully, it allows us to begin and wrap up our days with a sense of presence and calmness.

Instead of being lost in thought and worries when you brush your teeth, gently bring your attention back to the sensations of brushing each time you realize that your mind has wandered off. Focusing on your various senses is a great way to break the habit of overthinking and come back to the present moment, not only when brushing your teeth but throughout your day in whatever task you're doing. What do you see? What can you hear? How does the toothpaste smell? What does it taste like?

Then move on to start becoming aware of the sensations that you're experiencing. Feel the bristles against your teeth and gums. Feel the movement of your arm as you're brushing. If you want to challenge yourself, use your non-dominant hand for brushing. Notice any other sensations. As you brush, be grateful for your teeth and everything they do for you every day.

A lot of things we do in life, like brushing our teeth, showering, and eating, can become routine, and we can sometimes go into autopilot. I challenge you to avoid autopilot by being as present as possible with each task you do throughout the day. Doing so will allow you to be fully present with whomever you're with.

If you want to strengthen your "presence muscle" even more, I highly recommend that you also include the formal mindfulness pieces of training into your life.

Formal Mindfulness Practices

Meditation
If you want to increase your ability to be more present in your life and receive many other benefits, such as decreasing stress and anxiety and greater focus and happiness, then I suggest you give meditation a try. This way, you can find out for yourself why so many busy executives, professional athletes, entrepreneurs, and parents are making meditation a priority in their daily lives.

Instructions
When: If possible, find the same time every day to practise your seated mindfulness meditation. Mornings or before bed are both great times to practise.

Where: Find a space at home that is quiet and comfortable for you to meditate—it could be sitting on a cushion or a chair. Leave this space set up and come back to this same place to meditate daily. Throughout your day, you can also meditate anywhere, including on the train, a park bench, at your desk, etc.

How: Sit with a straight yet relaxed back. Focus on the sensation of your breath flowing in and out. If you like, you can breathe in a feeling of calm and breathe out a sense of ease. When your mind wanders off or gets distracted, just let go of the thought or the distraction and then come back to the awareness of your breath flowing in and out. Be sure to do this without judging yourself; be kind, gentle, and compassionate. Imagine that your mind is a new puppy that you're teaching to sit for the first time.

How long: Begin meditating for a minimum of three minutes daily and then slowly increase the length of your meditation over time to fifteen minutes (or longer if you choose). If you're not using a guided meditation, make sure to set a timer so you can fully immerse yourself and lose track of time. Aim for daily-ish meditation practice. Intend to meditate every day (just like flossing your teeth), but if you miss a day, don't worry about it and get back on track the next day.

Recommended guided meditations: When you first start meditating, it is often easier to stay focused if you use a guided meditation. You can find numerous guided meditations on YouTube, podcasts, or various apps. Two apps that I often recommend are HeadSpace and Calm. You are welcome to download my own guided meditations by going to balancequest.com and then clicking on "Free Guided Meditations." At the time of writing, I've had over 100,000 downloads of these meditations.

Body Scan
The following mini seated body scan can be done in a minute or two anytime throughout the day. It's a great way to take a break when you've been working on your computer for a long time. Practising the body scan will help to bring your mind back to your body, relax your body, and help you to feel more present. You could do a quick body scan before you have a Talk2MorePeople interaction to help you feel more relaxed and present.

Instructions: Begin by becoming aware of any tension that you may be holding in your jaw or anywhere else in your face. Take a deep breath in, and then exhale and release the tension in your jaw and face. Try relaxing your jaw even more by opening your mouth slightly or by smiling. When you smile, it's like doing yoga for your face, and it relaxes your face and makes you feel better.

Now bring your awareness to your neck and shoulders. Take a deep breath in, and as you exhale, relax your shoulders down away from your ears. Letting go of the weight of the world and responsibilities that you sometimes carry around on your shoulders.

Become aware of any tension in your arms, hands, and fingers. Take a deep breath in, breathe out, and release that tension and let it evaporate away.

Scan down your back and notice any tension. If you notice any tension anywhere in your back, imagine breathing into that area, creating space and as you exhale, relax and let go of any stress or discomfort in your back.

Bring your awareness to the weight of your hips on the chair. Scan down your legs and become aware of your feet on the floor. Take a deep breath and then, as you exhale, let go of any tension from your lower body. Feel this sense of becoming grounded and present.

You can also practise the body scan while lying down. Starting with either your feet or your head, you scan up or down your body noticing tension, breathing into the area of stress, and then, as you exhale, relax your body onto the bed or floor below you. The body scan is a great tool to use to help you fall asleep.

Having a daily meditation practice and integrating the informal mindfulness practices into my life have helped me find more peace, contentment, and joy. These powerful practices have been around for thousands of years, and that's because they work. My wish is that you start to bring more mindfulness into your life and that these practices help you to live a healthier and happier life. Then you can ripple that happiness out into the world as you Talk2MorePeople.

NOTES

1. Matthew Lieberman explores human beings' need for interpersonal connection in his book *Social: Why Our Brains Are Wired to Connect* (New York: Crown, 2013). Also check out the his conversation with *Scientific American*, "Why We Are Wired to Connect" (October 22, 2013): https://www.scientificamerican.com/article/why-we-are-wired-to-connect/.

2. Gillian Sandstrom explains her findings in Chris Bourn's article "Why Talking to Strangers Is the Best Thing You Can Do for Your Mental Health," *MEL Magazine* (2019): https://melmagazine.com/en-us/story/why-talking-to-strangers-is-the-best-thing-you-can-do-for-your-mental-health and on her own site, https://gilliansandstrom.com/talking2strangers_research/.

3. According to Lisa Fritscher in her article "Fear of Rejection and its Consequences" for Verywell Mind (November 7, 2019), there are four common behaviours in those who have a fear of rejection (https://www.verywellmind.com/what-is-the-fear-of-rejection-2671841). I have seen each of them in myself at different times of my life. They are phoniness, people-pleasing, unassertiveness, and passive-aggressiveness. You may or may not exhibit these behaviours, and you may or may not be aware if you do.

4. Nicholas Epley and Juliana Schroeder, "Mistakenly Seeking Solitude," *Journal of Experimental Psychology* 143, no. 5 (2014): 1984, http://dx.doi.org/10.1037/a0037323.

5. Epley and Schroeder, "The Surprising Benefits of Talking to Strangers," *The Guardian* (June 12, 2019): https://www.bbc.co.uk/news/world-48459940.

6. For more information on rejection therapy, check out Harriet Lerner's article "The Fear of Rejection: A One-Day Cure! (Part I)" for *Psychology Today* (March 27, 2010): https://www.psychologytoday.com/us/blog/the-dance-connection/201003/the-fear-rejection-one-day-cure-part-i.

7. Explore this research to learn how even just receiving a notification but not responding to it has a cost for your productivity. Cary Stothart, Ainsley Mitchum, and Courtney Yehnert, "The Attentional Cost of Receiving a Cell Phone Notification," *Journal of Experimental Psychology Human Perception & Performance* (June 2015): 9, https://www.researchgate.net/publication/279457726.

8. The source of these statistics is Simon Kemp's summary of We Are Social and Hootsuite's collection of Global Digital 2019 reports in "Digital 2019: Global Internet Use Accelerates," We Are Social (January 30, 2019): https://wearesocial.com/blog/2019/01/digital-2019-global-internet-use-accelerates.

9. Melissa Hunt, Rachel Marx, Courtney Lipson, and Jordyn Young, "No More FOMO: Limiting Social Media Decreases Loneliness and Depression," *Journal of Social and Clinical Psychology* 37, no. 10 (2018): 763, 766, 767.

10. Gustavo Razzetti, "How to Overcome the Fear of Change," *Psychology Today* (September 18, 2018): https://www.psychologytoday.com/ca/blog/the-adaptive-mind/201809/how-overcome-the-fear-change. Razzetti is the author of *Stretch for Change* (USA: Liberationist Press, 2017).

11. Check out my video from Day 1 of the Talk2MorePeople Project (Piccadilly Circus, London, England) on YouTube at https://youtu.be/KRQ3rU0IkBo.

12. See Melanie Curtin's article, "Are You on Your Phone Too Much? The Average Person Spends This Many Hours on It Every Day," Inc.com (October 30, 2018): https://www.inc.com/melanie-curtin/are-you-on-your-phone-too-much-average-person-spends-this-many-hours-on-it-every-day.html.

13. Check out Alice Park's article, "Too Much Screen Time Can Have Lasting Consequences for Young Children's Brains," *Time* (January 28, 2019): https://time.com/5514539/screen-time-children-brain/.

14. For more information, read the article "Role of Play in Social Skills and Intelligence of Children," *Procedia: Social and Behavioral Sciences* 30 (2011): 2272–2279.

15. See Matthias Gruber's article "States of Curiosity Modulate Hippocampus-Dependent Learning via the Dopaminergic Circuit," *Neuron* 84, no. 2 (2014): 486–496. https://www.cell.com/neuron/fulltext/S0896-6273(14)00804-6.

16. See Jane Fonda's acceptance speech at the American Film Institute's Life Achievement Award ceremony in June 2014 (*The Daily Star*, June 7, 2014: https://www.thedailystar.net/jane-fonda-honoured-by-hollywood-stars-27324).

17. Francesca Gino, "The Business Case for Curiosity," *Harvard Business Review* (September–October 2018): https://hbr.org/2018/09/curiosity.

18. The first three benefits are listed in Emily Campbell's "Six Surprising Benefits of Curiosity," *Greater Good Magazine* (September 24, 2015): https://greatergood.berkeley.edu/article/item/six_surprising_benefits_of_curiosity. The mental stimulation resulting from curiosity is explored in Denise Ahlquist's post, "Achieve Better Learning: Utilize Curiosity to Stimulate Brain Function," Getting Smart (August 11, 2017): https://www.gettingsmart.com/2017/08/achieve-better-learning-utilize-curiosity-to-stimulate-brain-function/.

19. Leon Seltzer, "The Wisdom of Spontaneity (Part 2)," *Psychology Today* (April 3, 2009): https://www.psychologytoday.com/us/blog/evolution-the-self/200904/the-wisdom-spontaneity-part-2.

20. See "3 Keys to Being More Spontaneous," Exploring Your Mind (February 5, 2018): https://exploringyourmind.com/3-keys-to-being-more-spontaneous/.

21. Check out Michael Formica's "5 Steps for Being Present," *Psychology Today* (June 14, 2011): https://www.psychologytoday.com/ca/blog/enlightened-living/201106/5-steps-being-present.

22. If you would like an in-depth look at the difference between informal and formal mindfulness practices, check out the following study: Kelly Birtwell, Kate Williams, Harm van Marwijk, Christopher J. Armitage, and David Sheffield, "An Exploration of Formal and Informal Mindfulness Practice and Associations with Wellbeing," *Mindfulness* 10 (2019): 89–99, https://rdcu.be/b3Qi0.

23. I learned this fact from Tracey Delfs (BalanceQuest.ca/), who has a full mindfulness section for you in the Appendix.

24. Adrian F. Ward, Kristen Duke, Ayelet Gneezy, and Maarten W. Bos, "Brain Drain: The Mere Presence of One's Own Smartphone Reduces Available Cognitive Capacity," *Journal of the Association of Consumer Research* 2, no. 2 (2017): https://www.journals.uchicago.edu/doi/full/10.1086/691462.

25. Linda Graham, "Mitigate the Stress Response with a Hand on Your Heart," Love and Life Toolbox: https://loveandlifetoolbox.com/mitigate-the-stress-response-with-a-hand-on-your-heart/.

26. Here are 10 tips on how to slow down from the World Institute of Slowness: https://www.theworldinstituteofslowness.com/10-ways/. My favourite from their list is "Don't multitask."

27. If you believe the people in your city are extra unfriendly, you likely live in a big city. And if that's true, then there will be thousands of friendly people living amongst the unfriendly people. You just need to find them. Using this excuse is just a self-limiting belief. See Todd Kashdan's article "The Mental Benefits of Vacationing Somewhere New," *Harvard Business Review* (January 26, 2018): https://hbr.org/2018/01/the-mental-benefits-of-vacationing-somewhere-new.

28. J. Holt-Lunstad, T.B. Smith, M. Baker, T. Harris, and D. Stephenson, "Loneliness and Social Isolation as Risk Factors for Mortality: A Meta-Analytic Review," *Perspectives on Psychological Science* 10 (2015): 227-237.

29. For a captivating peek into the night circus, which the circus that I perform in (Le Cirque de la Nuit) was inspired by, spend time with the book *The Night Circus* by Erin Morgenstern. Allow yourself to get swept away with this novel. When you return from your adventure, see if you can create some magic of your own with the people you encounter.

30. Visit https://www.CirqueNuit.com/.

31. For more information about other types of listening, including appreciative, comprehensive, and critical listening, check out the following sources: Ben Janse, "Appreciative Listening," *ToolsHero* (Novemeber 14, 2018): www.toolshero.com/communication-skills/appreciative-listening/; "5 Types of Listening to Become an Awesome Listener," Udemy (February 2020): https://blog.udemy.com/types-of-listening/.

32. Watch the Netflix film *The Social Dilemma* for a deeper look at how these companies have made it so hard for us to put down the devices.

33. For more about our response to notifications, read Alexia Lafata's article "Generation Notification: Why Our Brains Literally Love Notifications," *Elite Daily* (December 8, 2014): https://www.elitedaily.com/life/generation-notification-science-behind-notifications-obsessed/866812.

34. Check out "Is 'Selective Hearing' Actually a Thing?" Health24 (December 7, 2017): https://www.health24.com/Medical/Hearing-management/Anatomy-of-hearing/is-selective-hearing-actually-a-thing-20160617.

35. Christian Jarrett, "Why Meeting Another's Gaze Is So Powerful," Future (January 8, 2019): https://www.bbc.com/future/article/20190108-why-meeting-anothers-gaze-is-so-powerful.

36. For more information about active listening, visit https://www.skillsyouneed.com/ips/active-listening.html.

37. These five empathetic listening tips are from Jaya Ramchandani's article "What Is Empathetic Listening?" *Medium* (July 15, 2018): https://medium.com/we-learn-we-grow/what-is-empathic-listening-34a164f572a0.

38. Check out Starr Sackstein's book *Teaching Students to Self-Assess* (Alexandria, Virginia: Association for Supervision and Curriculum Development, 2015).

39. Watch my video of one pandemic information gift exchange on YouTube: https://www.youtube.com/watch?v=o0FqxpHZdoM&lc=Ugw0Z2nOuB6knFh1_HF4AaABAg.

40. Watch Brené Brown's blockbuster TED talk, "The Power of Vulnerability": https://www.ted.com/talks/brene_brown_the_power_of_vulnerability?language=en.

41. Kio Stark, When Strangers Meet: How People You Don't Know Can Transform You (New York: Simon & Schuster/TED, 2016), 93.

42. Hara Estroff Marano, "The Art of the Compliment," *Psychology Today* (March 1, 2004): https://www.psychologytoday.com/ca/articles/200403/the-art-the-compliment#.

43. Please see my video, November Project Calgary Introduction, at youtube.com/watch?v=4pu7cWiweY8.

44. See Jill Suttie and Jason Marsh's article "5 Ways Giving Is Good for You," *Greater Good Magazine* (December 13, 2010): https://greatergood.berkeley.edu/article/item/5_ways_giving_is_good_for_you.

45. Stephen Post, "It's Good to Be Good: 2014 Biennial Scientific Report on Health, Happiness, Longevity, and Helping Others," *International Journal of Person Centered Medicine* 2 (2014): 1–53.

46. See "The Alberta Men's Survey," Alberta Men's Network (July–October 2015): http://www.albertamen.com/results.

47. Heidi Grant's work is discussed in Angela Chen's article "A Social Psychologist Explains Why We Should Ask for Help More Often," *The Verge* (June 22, 2018): https://www.theverge.com/2018/6/22/17475134/heidi-grant-reinforcements-help-social-psychology.

48. Alison Wood Brooks and Francesca Gino, "Asking Advice Makes a Good Impression," *Scientific American* (October 7, 2014): https://www.scientificamerican.com/article/asking-advice-makes-a-good-impression/.

49. Chen, "A Social Psychologist Explains Why We Should Ask for Help More Often." https://www.f3nws.com/news/a-social-psychologist-explains-why-we-should-ask-for-help-more-often-ec670087.

50. John Corcoran, "How to Follow Up After Meeting Someone in Person," The Art of Manliness (August 8, 2013): https://www.artofmanliness.com/articles/how-to-follow-up-after-meeting-someone-in-person/.

51. Watch the video from Day 79 of the Talk2MorePeople Project on YouTube at https://www.youtube.com/watch?v=yiES8kP8y7M.

52. Khalil Smith, Heidi Grant, and David Rock, "How to Speak Up When It Matters," *Harvard Business Review* (March 4, 2019): https://hbr.org/2019/03/how-to-speak-up-when-it-matters. For another resource on this subject, check out Susan Biali's "How to Speak Up for Yourself with Wisdom and Courage," *Psychology Today* (September 4, 2018): https://www.psychologytoday.com/ca/blog/prescriptions-life/201809/how-speak-yourself-wisdom-and-courage.

53. University of Tennessee at Knoxville, "Psychologists Find Smiling Really Can Make People Happier," *ScienceDaily* (April 12, 2019): https://www.sciencedaily.com/releases/2019/04/190412094728.htm.

54. See Stuart Brown's article "Play Deprivation...A Leading Indicator for Mass Murder," The National Institute for Play (June 1, 2014): http://www.nifplay.org/blog/play-deprivation-a-leading-indicator-for-mass-murder/.

55. Visit https://foursightonline.com.

56. To read Mike's blogpost, "A Tribute to My Dad, Gord!" (November 25, 2016), visit https://mikesmailbag.org/2016/11/mikes-mailbag-a-tribute-to-my-dad-gord/. Mike and I connected after he read the following article about me: "Calgary Man 7 Months into Challenge to Meet New People Every Day," CBC News (October 24, 2016): https://www.cbc.ca/news/canada/calgary/calgary-man-talk-2-more-people-1.3814461.

57. To learn more about leadership and improvisation, and how to apply it to your everyday life, The Second City book *Yes, And: How Improvisation Reverses "No, But" Thinking and Improves Creativity and Collaboration* is a very worthwhile read.

58. "The Campaign to End Loneliness" (https://www.campaigntoendloneliness.org) is a great UK resource on loneliness. Take a look at their extensive research on the subject and sign up for free resources to support you or someone who you know could benefit.

59. Gillian Sandstrom and Erica J. Boothby, "Why Do People Avoid Talking to Strangers? A Mini Meta-Analysis of Predicted Fears and Actual Experiences Talking to a Stranger," *Self and Identity* (2020): 38–39.

60. To see my Last 30 Days of 30s videos, check out https://bit.ly/2IkfUVN.

61. For support getting focused on your 30-Day Challenge or any other important project, I suggest reading the book *The One Thing: The Surprising Simple Truth Behind Extraordinary Results* (Portland, Oregon: Bard Press, 2013) by Gary Keller and Jay Papasan. This book has helped me learn how to time-block to get better results in many different projects.

62. I have my friend Kate McKenzie to thank for suggesting I create a card. She told me before I began the project, "If you want to make an impact with an idea, you need to have something that people can engage with." That inspired the creation of the 30-Day Challenge card. Take a look at the incredible work Kate McKenzie and Martin Parnell are doing with their book and award-winning documentary, *The Secret Marathon*, at https://thesecretmarathon.com/. They also created the Secret 3K runs that happen all over the world during International Women's Week. These events support and promote gender equality and accessibility to sports. Kate sets an inspiring example of how an idea can engage thousands of people for positive change. She ran her first-ever marathon in Afghanistan while producing a documentary about it. Talk about a challenge! If Kate could manage all of that, then you can likely meet a few new people this week.

63. Thich Nhat Hanh, *Be Still and Know: Reflections from Living Buddha, Living Christ* (New York: Riverhead, 2016), 19.

64. Florida State University, "Chore or Stress Reliever: Study Suggests That Washing Dishes Decreases Stress," *ScienceDaily* (October 1, 2015): https://www.sciencedaily.com/releases/2015/10/151001165852.htm.

65. Thich Nhat Hanh, Dharma Talk at Plum Village Mindfulness Retreat Centre, France, January 2010.

66. Thich Nhat Hanh, *The Long Road Turns to Joy: A Guide to Walking Meditation* (Berkeley, California: Parallax Press, 2011), 90.

OTHER RESOURCES

Websites That Have Changed My Life and Could Change Yours

- Couchsurfing.org: A global travellers' community where people stay with and host strangers from around the world. Through this network I have met fellow travellers and joined in on various adventures.

- Gilliansandstrom.com: Website of Gillian Sandstrom, PhD. Explore the resources on talking to strangers on her website.

- Heidigrantphd.com: Website of Heidi Grant, PhD. Watch her TED talk on how to ask for help and grab excellent resources from her website.

- HoffmanInstitute.ca: A place where people go to eliminate their negative patterns of belief through the Hoffman Process. My process was in 2017 and I will forever be grateful for what I experienced there. I learned how to love myself for who I am.

- LivingRoomSeries.me: A place created "to gather people with different backgrounds to expand everyone's perspective through words and stories." This is a great place for meaningful conversations.

- Meetup.com: An online network to find people with similar interests in thousands of cities all around the world to meet up offline.

- SofarSounds.com: A platform where local artists perform their music in private homes to attentive audiences.

- TED.com: A source for thousands of incredible ideas.

- Toastmasters.org: A leadership organization with thousands of locations around the world. It teaches in-person communication skills. I learned from attending Toastmasters meetings for more than two years. Here is a great resource on body language: *Dimensions on Body Language*, westsidetoastmasters.com/resources/book_of_body_language/toc.html.

- WinWenger.com: A collection of incredible and unique creative problem-solving techniques that utilize the powerful unconscious mind. I have had the privilege of studying these techniques directly from Dr. Wenger and can tell you that he is a kind, warm-hearted creative genius. You can learn from his work.

Books That Have Changed My Direction and Could Change Yours

- Nir Eyal, *Indistractable: How to Control Your Attention and Choose Your Life* (Dallas: BanBella Books, Inc, 2019).

- Michael Gelb and Tony Buzan, *Lessons from the Art of Juggling: How to Achieve Your Full Potential in Business, Learning, and Life* (New York: Harmony, 1994).

- Darren Hardy, *The Compound Effect: Jumpstart Your Income, Your Life, Your Success* (Vanguard Press, 2012).

- Esther Hicks and Jerry Hicks, *Ask and It Is Given: Learning to Manifest Your Desires,* (Carlsbad, California: Hay House, 2004).

- Thomas King, *An Inconvenient Indian: A Curious Account of Native People in North America* (Toronto: Anchor Canada, 2013).

- Richard Koch and Greg Lockwood, *Superconnect: Harnessing the Power of Networks and the Strength of Weak Links* (New York: Norton, 2010).

- Erin Morgenstern, *The Night Circus* (New York: Random House, 2012).

- Steven Pressfield, *The War of Art: Break Through the Blocks and Win Your Inner Creative Battles* (Black Irish Entertainment LLC, 2011).

- Douglas Rushkoff, *Team Human* (New York: Douglas Rushkoff, 2019).

- Lance Secretan, *The Spark, the Flame and the Torch: Inspire Self. Inspire Others. Inspire the World* (Caledon, Ontario: Secretan Center Inc., 2010).

- Michael Bungay Stanier, *The Coaching Habit: Say Less, Ask More and Change the Way You Lead Forever* (Vancouver: Page Two, 2016).

- Danny Wallace, *Yes Man* (New York: Simon & Schuster, 2006).

- Win Wenger and Richard Poe, *The Einstein Factor: A Proven New Method for Increasing Your Intelligence* (Prima Publishing, 1996).

Miscellaneous

- Loneliness is an epidemic in society today and is now a minister-level job in the UK: gov.uk/government/news/pm-launches-governments-first-loneliness-strategy.

- Friend and colleague Patricia Morgan is a resiliency expert and a spunky senior. Patricia is the youngest person in her seventies that I know. Explore her extensive website with resiliency resources at SolutionsforResilience.com.

- You have heard a few references to a mirror suit and reflections throughout the book. That's because someone I met on Day 200 of the project, Olga Sem, custom made me that mirror suit. She is a talented mask and costume designer and her work can be seen at Instagram.com/OlgaSemMasks. For more reflections, visit Instagram.com/MirrorManYYC or take a closer look at the cover of this book.

- Explore these 150 Acts of Reconciliation "to think about Indigenous-settler relationships in new ways. We encourage you to use #150Acts to share your engagement with each item on the list": activehistory.ca/2017/08/150-acts-of-reconciliation-for-the-last-150-days-of-canadas-150/.

- Watch my tutorial on how to juggle: youtu.be/AF7QFq9Cjak.

- Check out Hall of Fame business speaker Michael Kerr, author of *The Humor Advantage*, and a podcast for workplace research and a lot of fun. Visit Mikekerr.com/category/podcast-humor-at-work.

- Watch this TEDxYYC talk with no words with Le Cirque de la Nuit, "The Creative Process": youtu.be/oq4ZMriqSM8.

- Visit Mindcamp.org to join an international online creativity community called Mindcamp Connect.

- Search online for "Wildfit with Ginny Santos" to get coached on how to remove all pain from your body (as I experienced) and achieve food freedom through a transformational 90-day challenge.

- Teamkind.org.uk is an organization that you can join to create more kindness in the world. Be sure to attend their next virtual kindness festival.

Just for Fun

This is an incomplete list of things that I do just for fun. You can practise some or all of these to bring more playfulness into your life.

- Joke around with people daily. Play with words and drop puns.

- Ask *a lot* of questions everywhere, all the time.

- Use your phone when you need it and keep it away most of the time.

- Surprise friends and family members with playful pranks when you get the chance, understanding that there may be playful payback.

- Smile every day.

- Speak in different accents in public.

- Play Ping-Pong or miniPong.

- Meet new people with excitement and enthusiasm.

- Climb on things in public.

- Search for and join an in-person or virtual cypher club to practice your freestyle skills.

- Play games with children when you get the opportunity to.

- Participate in improv theatre nights or jams and do improv games often.

- Juggle, dance, do yoga, and balance on a slackline.

- Spend more time in nature and, if you can, in the mountains.

- Allow yourself to laugh out loud.

ABOUT THE AUTHOR

 International facilitator, performing artist, and solution-focused coach Tony Esteves is passionate about creating human connection, going up or down mountains, and setting off on adventures. He holds a Bachelor of Arts in communication studies, intentionally meets new people regularly, and loves to read, write, play and improvise. He exists in Calgary, Alberta, Canada.

Having lived, worked, or travelled in forty countries, he has facilitated learning experiences in North America, Europe, and South Africa and learned a few languages along the way. He found himself working on a US military base in Uzbekistan for a while and has only been kicked out of Hungary once.

He created the Talk2MorePeople Project, which evolved into a year-long journey of human connection. In that year Tony met over 550 strangers, and his mental health, and life, were transformed. He shares his insights with groups who value entertaining learning experiences and meaningful conversations. Meeting a stranger is how he joined the circus and it's why he has a mirror suit.

Join Tony's adventure to help put an end to the epidemic of loneliness in the world today at Talk2MorePeople.com, or find him @Talk2MorePeople. For meaningful content on human connection, and upcoming publications and performances, join his newsletter at tinyurl.com/T2MPnews.

*Please cut out, copy, or take a photo of a card
and use it as a tool to meet people today.*

	Sun	Mon	Tue	Wed	Thurs	Fri	Sat

30-Day Challenge

"Excuse me, I just overheard you say..."
"May I ask you a quick question?"
"Excuse me, may I help you with that?"

Meet a person,
tick a box. ✓

	Sun	Mon	Tue	Wed	Thurs	Fri	Sat

30-Day Challenge

"Excuse me, I just overheard you say..."
"May I ask you a quick question?"
"Excuse me, may I help you with that?"

Meet a person,
tick a box. ✓

	Sun	Mon	Tue	Wed	Thurs	Fri	Sat

30-Day Challenge

"Excuse me, I just overheard you say..."
"May I ask you a quick question?"
"Excuse me, may I help you with that?"

Meet a person,
tick a box. ✓

@Talk2MorePeople

L Listen

O Overcome Internal Obstacles

O Open a Dialogue

K Keep (the Conversation) Going

U Uncomfortable? How to Exit a Conversation

P Play and Improvise

@Talk2MorePeople

L Listen

O Overcome Internal Obstacles

O Open a Dialogue

K Keep (the Conversation) Going

U Uncomfortable? How to Exit a Conversation

P Play and Improvise

@Talk2MorePeople

L Listen

O Overcome Internal Obstacles

O Open a Dialogue

K Keep (the Conversation) Going

U Uncomfortable? How to Exit a Conversation

P Play and Improvise